Stop It!

STOP TRYING TO BECOME WHO YOU ALREADY ARE.

by Sheri Yates

IDNJC

Publisher iKAN Publish.com

Stop IT!
Stop trying to become who you already are.
by Sheri Yates
Copyright © 2016 by Sheri Yates

I would love to hear from you.
www.ikanministries.com

ISBN-13: 978-1530818587
ISBN-10: 1530818583

Cover:
Interior design:
Editor: Adam M. Swiger
Wordsmith: Rebecca Bugger

All Scripture quotations, unless otherwise indicated, are taken from the Holy Bible, New International Version (NIV).

Printed in the United States of America.

Acknowledgements

It's just crazy the team I had for this book because I have never met three of them! God has literally formed my team for me with people that love and support me in ways I could have never imagined. They are from all over the globe! I love them all.

Adam…Thank you for being such a faithful editor of all things over the past year! Never met you, but madly respect you!

Rebecca…Girl, you can write. Thank you for making my book sound better than I could ever write! I love your humor and fun style. You make me better!

Nona…I am so grateful to have you as my assistant! I cannot tell you how much you have blessed my life this past 15 months! You know my most intimate thoughts because you type them all for me! I praise God for you.

Kathleen…Thank you for busting your pen (on the airplane) with excitement over this book. It seriously kicked me in the pants and ignited my fire to finish it!

Ty…Thank you for believing in me and funding my dreams. You are the most supportive husband ever. Thank you for allowing me to word vomit daily on my computer, recorder, and in your ear. I love you!

I am thankful for Jesus and the TRUTH that God is the ONLY truth I need – and Every man is a liar – including myself! Because of His Truth paving new highways in my mind, I am not a remnant of that lost, sad, seeking little girl I was for so many years! Hallelujah!

Dedication

To Spencer, Chandler, Kennedi, Katie Candle, Steph, Taylor, Jett, Kathleen, Lizzie, Kyle, and my future nieces and nephews and grandbabies, and my much younger cousins Ashton, Kylie, Jacob, Kendyl, Kamryn, Crayton, Jensen, Sydney, Amberger, Tommy, and MyLee, my girl's friends, Original Design Youth Group, my Avodah Family, iKAN team, Truth Group, and all the people I love so much – may you never settle for lies about your identity. You were born for an abundant life! Always trust who God says you are! Let God be true and every man a liar – including yourself!

To Spencer, Chandler and Kennedi I love you more than you can possibly comprehend! Because of you, I daily desire to become more like a child to have faith like yours! Each of you inspire me!

Ty – I cannot believe I get to be your wife! It's truly an honor!

From the Author

Stop trying to become who you already are. Excuse me while I preach to myself.

I literally repeat this line quite frequently. I will be the first to admit that I have not arrived. I do not live out of my identity perfectly. I struggle. Daily, I have to choose to not take up an offense at people, my family, etc.

The battle is real. Sometimes I am victorious… Sometimes I am not. I can tell you that laying down my old identity, my life, my pride (like I deserve something better) can often be a tough decision.

Sometimes I want to throw a big ole' adult brat fit. I would like to chew someone out for being thoughtless, inconsiderate, and exclusive… You name it – and I have unleashed fury when I have been hurt.

Even though I fail, in Christ I am still perfect in his eyes. I am imperfect… Imperfectly perfect.

There is a battle. It's a battle between unity and division. It's between love and rejection. There are so many facets of this battle to thwart us from continuously living out of the love Christ died for us to display while on this earth.

The question isn't "When will we arrive at perfection?" because you will have to die to achieve that.

The real question is: Will you engage in the battle? Will you say yes to learn how to truly live in the fullness of your identity in Christ? The commitment isn't easy. It's a constant decision to fight for daily.

Saying yes will change your life. Regardless of how people feel about you, you will now be in a position to choose joy regardless.

All that you've been striving to be, you already are. You are more than you know you are. It's found in Jesus. It's all yours, but you must take possession of it. It's time to stop it! Stop trying to become who you already are and learn to walk in it.

You are not a failure even though you have failed. You are strong when you are weak. In Christ, you are imperfectly perfect. You can choose to believe in yourself because God already believes in you!

I am so thankful that I had the opportunity to write this book because I pray it pushes your limits so that you can find a new height in HIM!

How many times do you think like this:

- What is wrong with me?
- Why am I so stupid?
- I am fat and pudgy.
- I am ugly.
- I have nothing to wear.
- I am not successful enough.
- I am a failure.

Although these may be factual, in Christ, none of those things are TRUE! Truth is what God says – Period.

Why then do you and I speak of facts and circumstances more than we speak God's truth? It is because circumstances can be more real to us than the God's word.

It is time for us to stop it! In Christ, God, His Word, and His promises should be more reality than our feelings or circumstance. Let me repeat that: You and I need to

Stop believing an inferior view of yourself and start seeing yourself as God sees you!

Sounds so easy. I know right?!

It's about as easy as getting fit. You only have to start! Pry your booty from the sofa, hit the gym, eat clean, and do it 5-7 days a week for the remainder of your life. Once you begin to see your energy, body, and attitude improve, you wonder why you didn't do it sooner. You can stop viewing everything in your life as a victim and start viewing yourself as the victor you are in Christ today or next year – or never. You will never regret starting. You will only regret the continued pain of allowing everything that happens to you to hold you in slavery.

No more. Let us all begin right now. Stop it – the delay – putting it off – and stop right now. Establish a time to read this book, your Bible and this will be your first step like pushing yourself off the couch to workout!

Set a specific time to take possession of your True ID! I suggest something like this: After breakfast, I will spend 15 minutes taking possession of who God says I am.

> *Write it here. Date it and sign it. Commit to this. Tab this page to remind yourself daily.*
>
> _____
> _____
> _____
> _____
> _____
> _____

Here's an overview of our journey together:
- Believe who He says you are.
- Exercise your mind to receive His Truth.
- Change your speech to agree with God's heart toward you – meaning stop speaking junk about yourself!

Your mind is programmed by repetitive thoughts and words you hear and speak. Remember that faith comes by hearing, so it is time to stop rattling off and venting about your problems, past, and your negative thoughts because it is no longer the person you are in Christ! You are more than the sum of the things you have done.

No one desires to lose their driver's license or have their ID stolen, but now is the time to lose your old ID. Refuse to continue to live out of who you were. Lay down the old labels, nicknames, or anything that someone marked you with that became part of your being.

Take possession of your new IDNJC (Identity in Jesus Christ!). The blood of Jesus has marked you. Your old labels are gone – even though you will probably continue to struggle! You have been given a new name in the family of God. You have been adopted. The Bible is your adoption manual. Your bloodline and legacy is now rooted in the blood of Jesus!

Now it's time for you and I to overcome freedom from any remnant of our old identities. We are going to take possession of our IDNJC using our adoption manuals!! Let us do this!

Love,
Sheri Yates

> *Believe who He says you are. It's the most humble thing you will ever do.*

Table of Contents

Introduction 1

Identify It! 3

Heal It! 13

Treasure It! 23

Fight It! 35

Reveal It! 43

Believe It! 53

Take It! 63

Adopt It! 71

See It! 79

Stop It! 87

Start It! 95

Start It The Achievable Proverbs 31 Woman 103

Introduction

So often we talk about the pressures that are placed on teenage girls to look and act a certain way. Yes, those pressures exist, but it's not just those teeny-boppers that can feel the weight of the world on their shoulders. (Especially after a Krispy Kreme donut or two…) The pressure is everywhere. Be a perfect parent. Have a perfect family. Achieve a successful career. Cook like Pioneer Woman but figure out how to not look like you've been eating her food. It's overwhelming, imminent and impossible all at once. How many times do you catch yourself talking negatively about your body, hair, self? What's your identity? Who are you? What do you tell yourself when you are alone in the dark? What is haunting you?

Do you think to yourself, *"What is wrong with me? I am so stupid! I am fat. So maybe I'm not fat, but I am totally pudgy. When did I get so wrinkly, ugly? I have nothing to wear. I am not successful enough. I am a failure. Why can't I get this right?"*

The truth is that when we are in Christ, none of those things can possibly be true. So why do we speak about circumstances more than we speak about truth? It has to be because we believe what we feel and we seem to feel our circumstances more than we feel God.

It's time to stop it!

It is time to stop settling for any view of ourselves except one. The view that *the One* has of us. The way God sees and knows us. He knows you best. It sounds so easy….right? Then make it easy! Start today! Get after it! Simply believe God.

What's funny is that I know that sounds impossible, but Jesus said in Mark 5:36, *"Don't be afraid; just believe."* Just believe God.

The reason it is so hard is because we have programmed our minds with our repetitive thoughts. Remember that faith comes by hearing. If you keep rattling off the old past, the old person, the identity you once had then you are hearing the wrong things. You are listening to yourself instead of God. It's time to STOP IT!

Identify It

Everyone has an identity. Some even have a secret identity. Sometimes that's a good thing. Sometimes it isn't. All of the time, you need to remember that you wouldn't be who you are today without that identity. It is sacred. You have to learn how to embrace it, let parts of it go, and mold it into exactly what God planned it to be. It took me a long time to embrace my identity, and it wasn't easy. But eventually I had to learn to leave it up to God, and you will too.

Our identity is formed at the beginning of our lives, when we don't even know it's happening. We are born and given a name. it is our identity. When I was born, I was given the name Sheri Dawn. From the very beginning of my life I was a case of mistaken identity. My name was supposed to be spelled Shari Dawn. The nurse misspelled it and my mom was so whipped out that she didn't take the time to correct it.

My mom wanted her independence from her large family of 8 children. She was the oldest and she was ready to stop babysitting and make her own way in the world. But back in 1960's, it wasn't typical for a woman to simply go make her way in the world on her own. My mom and dad were childhood sweethearts, the typical popular kids in school. They were married when they were only 19 years old. Smoking was a pretty big thing then, and my mom had starting smoking when she was just 14 years old. It made her feel older and more mature!

My parents were trying to find the "keys" to a happy marriage but neither of them even had the "keys" to their own identities. In the process, they discovered debt, drugs, the game of pool, and partying. Unfortunately, their lifestyle began to overtake their lives and became who they were. Before they knew it, they were selling drugs and traveling the country playing pool to support our family. I ran around in a diaper most of the time (which I didn't let my own children do because of that).

I know my parents loved me. They were just young. They had no vision for their lives other than freedom and happiness. Alcohol began to take control of my dad. It made him angry and abusive with my mom.

When I was three years old, I had such a fun spirit. It didn't matter who I was, it only mattered how I felt. And I felt happy! If you've ever been around a three-year-old, you know that they are the sweetest little things. Well, most of the time. I was a perfect angel, I'm sure. As an adult, I love to be around three-year-olds. They love and they're kind.

But at three years old, my dad was an alcoholic and he left our family. He left me at three. I couldn't comprehend why I wouldn't have a daddy anymore and that innate sense of happiness was crushed. He didn't actually get sober until I was an adult. I felt so rejected. I felt unloved and unworthy. It was so painful. Just as soon as I started to get my identity back, my mom got remarried and I had a stepdad, and I was hoping that we would have an awesome time together, maybe he would fill the void that had been left by my father.

I was partially right. My mom and stepdad had an awesome time. They were party animals, to say the least. I mean, my stepdad had a beard down to his belly, really long hair and looked like the epitome of a party guy. I'm pretty sure that they were drinking the majority of the time that they raised me. I'm sure that you can imagine that our home wasn't a very positive one.

I was blessed to spend time with my Grandma as well. She taught me to go to Church. I went to Church all by myself. I rode the Church bus everywhere I went. At ten years old, I raised my hand and gave my life to Christ and it was awesome. My parents couldn't understand. Later that exact same year, my identity was stolen from me in the middle of the night. I woke up and I found my stepdad in my bed. That night was the beginning of a four-year journey of losing my innocence, being violated in my own home. I didn't feel safe anymore.

I reflected, *"My life has been shattered. Who do I tell? What do I say? Can I tell my mom? If I tell my mom will she reject me, too? Is there something wrong with me?"*

I know what the statistics are. I know that I'm not the only person that that's happened to. I know what it does when you're hurt by someone. It creates so much shame that it steals your identity. You set on a mask. You start working hard to find something to cover the shame and the pain and you start working hard to be somebody that is lovable, somebody that is not trash. That is literally how I felt.

For years, I wore this giant mask. People believed, *"Oh my gosh! She's so fun. Sheri's great! I love her!"* I was a pompom girl with a really explosive personality. It was an excellent mask. The problem was that it was all fake. It was simply a cover up. It was my cover up because if anybody knew what had happened to me, I would die. I felt like it was my entire fault.

When you're abused, you don't know it, but the abuser wants you to feel that way. Like it's all your fault. My abuser was a pro. He started to mentally beat me up over and over again. He called me stupid for so long that I was still calling myself stupid until I was 26, when it finally broke. I thought I was stupid. I *believed* him.

I was set on a path of destruction. I needed to go find love. I needed to find something to fill me up. I was looking for that Jerry Maguire, *"you complete me"* kind of love. When I was 13 years old, my family got the chance to move. I was so completely excited to have a new home and a new place to live because, in the back of my mind, I believed that if I had a new home, maybe the abuse that's happened in my life won't happen anymore. Maybe the abuse that happened didn't really happen. Maybe I dreamed it. So, somehow, I thought this new home would be a new start, and that my entire circumstances would change. Shortly after we moved, I found out the hard way that it didn't change. I learned that, even though I had a new home, it didn't change any of my circumstances. They didn't go away.

That was when I realized that it wouldn't matter if I found that Jerry Maguire kind of love. I honestly believed my entire life that every person that I knew would eventually leave me. In fact, that's how I worked in relationships. If I thought you were being distant, I would leave first because I couldn't stand the

> *Are regrets dragging you down? You don't have time to maintain your regrets.*

thought of being rejected again. I couldn't handle the hurt. I protected myself. I was a sinner—and a notable one at that.

Have you ever felt like me? Have you ever felt that you're not good enough? Are you afraid of being rejected by someone else, maybe by a husband or a parent? Are you afraid of being rejected by your job? Are you worried about someone? Are you worried that maybe next month you won't be able to make the bills? Maybe you have an addiction that you cannot overcome. Maybe it's your regrets that are dragging you down.

> "FOR WE ARE GOD'S MASTERPIECE. HE HAS CREATED US ANEW IN CHRIST JESUS, SO WE CAN DO THE GOOD THINGS HE PLANNED FOR US LONG AGO."
>
> **Ephesians 2:10**

It took me a long time to realize that God said that I was chosen, holy and blameless and a masterpiece. Before I was born, he knew me and forgave me and that he restored me as if my sin, my past had never existed. It took me a long time to realize he did the same for my husband, that he did the same for my children. He did the same for you. That it's not entirely mine to have, but it's for every person I love and care about and I see around every corner.

Knowing my identity in Christ has truly freed me to see others as they are in Christ. I can look at them and claim, *"You know what; you are not the sum of what you've done. You're the sum of what He says."* I can look at someone in the middle of their dark, filthy sin and see them as chosen before that moment. When you're in the deepest despair in your life, when you're in the darkest sin that you chose to do, I can see that God loved you before, that he chose you, that you're his masterpiece. The only reason I'm freed up to see you like that, to see my husband like that, to see my children like that, is because I know God sees me like that. If he sees me like that, he has to see you like that. The scripture stated that he is no respecter of persons. One person doesn't have that identity and all the others don't. It's not the case. He has no favoritism. There's no favoritism in the kingdom of God.

You see, the world labels us. It sees us and defines us based on the things that we do or how we act or the talents and the gifts that we have. It will define us, embed labels on us, claim us and name us all day long. The world will give you names and tell you things like, *"Hey, you're a failure. You're a loser. These are your weaknesses. This is where you failed. You need to find something else to do for your career because you know what; you're not all of that and a bag of chips. You are not as special as you think you are. You need a different career path because God hasn't equipped you."*

> *Knowing my identity in Christ has not only set me free, but it has truly freed me to see others as they are in Christ too.*

And in essence, even in church, we tell people, *"You're too weak to do this job. You're not called to do this job. You're not equipped to do this job."* But then on the other side, we preach, *"God qualifies the called."* We declare, *"God is your strength and your weaknesses."* But yet, we turn people down and away every day because of how they are right at that moment and in their flesh.

We don't need to do that anymore. We need to stop and build people up in the truth. The more they know what their identity is, the more they know that God's strength fills their weaknesses. That takes them from a 50 to 100, from zero to a hero. God's strength takes the failure and makes him a successor. God's strength takes a pauper and makes him a king. God's strength makes your sin beautiful. Out of the ashes, he makes beauty. God's love takes someone who is unloving, unkind and makes them loving. God's love teaches you how to love the loveable.

God's love changes people. It changes people when you love people who are failing every day. God's love changes people who offend you. When you're offended, you can't love others. But when you know who you are in Christ and you know you're not somebody who takes offenses, you know that the love that is in you.

> "LOVE IS PATIENT, LOVE IS KIND. IT DOES NOT ENVY, IT DOES NOT BOAST, IT IS NOT PROUD. IT DOES NOT DISHONOR OTHERS, IT IS NOT SELF-SEEKING, IT IS NOT EASILY ANGERED, IT KEEPS NO RECORD OF WRONGS."
>
> **1 Corinthians 13:4**

It's a love that is not writing down, *"Here's where you failed and here's where your weaknesses are."* If we have God's kind of love, we shouldn't even be able to tell someone what they're doing wrong. Because you know what? A minute ago is the past.

> "FORGET THE FORMER THINGS AND SEE TODAY, I'M DOING A NEW THING."
>
> **Isaiah 43:18**

A minute ago is in the past. It's finished. When you know who you are in Christ, you'll forget the past. You'll forget a minute ago and immediately, you have new grace, new mercy for this person that you thought was a failure a minute ago and now you see them as God sees them. They are a masterpiece in Christ Jesus.

Learn to see through "Godggles" – God-goggles. God intends us to love others the way that he loves us. In second John, he says, *"To Gaius, whom I love in the truth."* In 3rd John, he calls, *"To the lady of"* whatever, *"whom I love in the truth."* The point of that is that he does not love them based on what they do, or what they've done or what they are; he loves them based on the truth. He's declaring, *"Through God's eye, I can love you fully."* You lack nothing through the eyes of God. You are the righteousness of God through Christ Jesus and I see you as righteous. I

When you know who you are in Christ, you'll forget the past.

don't care what you did, I see you as righteous. That is how to love with God's eyes.

I'm sure you're guilty like I am. You've labeled someone. You've caught someone in sin and you've labeled them. Or you've caught someone in failure and you've given them a title and declare to never trust them again. There's no way you're going to trust them with handling responsibility in the future. Maybe they failed you, maybe they quit on you. I think you see this with Mark and Paul in Barnabas. They had a feud. And you know what, Paul wouldn't trust again. He said, *"Let's go our separate ways and God can do something with that."* But in John 17, Jesus prayed for us to be one. He prayed that the body of Christ would be one vessel. He prayed that we would be in unity. There is no unity apart from seeing each other in true identity as brothers and sisters in Christ. We are aliens to this world. We are all in the same kingdom; we are all seated at the right hand with Jesus Christ.

I can't have unity with my brothers and sisters if I'm sitting there comparing and looking at their circumstance and behavior and I'm labeling them because of that. I'm choosing to say, *"You know what, they're not called or qualified. They're not able. They'll never get there. This isn't the right place for them. They're not on the right seat on the bus."* And I'm remembering, I'm keeping a record. I'm actually doing reviews.

Churches do reviews and tell people how they're doing. I think, every time, their record should be, *"You're a masterpiece, chosen, holy and blameless and God is your strength in the midst of your weaknesses."* This should be a suitable report. Yes, we could all improve on things, on the things that we do, but we are human beings, not human doings.

So, what is *your* identity? Is it real? Is it false?

A false identity is developed when you define yourself based off of anything other than God's truth. It isn't something that happens overnight. It happens slowly over time as we begin to believe the lies Satan and others tells us. Your false identity is deeply rooted and it's what you think and how you feel about yourself and not what God thinks of you.

- Your false identity places your identity in things. Examples of these "things" are your weaknesses, spiritual gifts, personality, titles, traits, positions, and strengths. Your identity is found in who God's says you are, not what He says you can do.
- Your false identity places your identity in people. You find it in being a mom of three kids, wife of a senator, daughter of married or divorced parents, etc. You know your identity is placed here when you believe that you will never be the same if you lost those people or your relationship with them changed.
- Your false identity makes you think that your identity is what should set you apart from others. Your real identity actually brings you together with other believers. What sets you apart and makes you unique are your spiritual gifts, personality, weaknesses and strengths.
- Your false identity makes you think you have to live up to certain standards. When validation from others is greater than the validation you receive from knowing who God says you are, you are placing your identity in something other than God's truth. You could spend a lifetime asking God to give you what you see others have. This is exactly what Satan desires you to do. He wants you to be jealous, insecure, and to covet what others have. He wants you to crave others' popularity, talent, personality, family, title and friends because it keeps the focus off of God and your reliance on Him.
- Your false identity lives in the past, thriving on what you did or was done to you. Those past experiences might be things such as death, bullying, sibling issues, eating disorders, divorce, infidelity, sickness, or abuse of any kind.

> *False identity places your identity in people, things, and performance. Your true identity is based solely on what God says.*

> "FOR BY YOUR WORDS YOU WILL BE JUSTIFIED, AND BY YOUR WORDS YOU WILL BE CONDEMNED."
>
> **Matthew 12:37**

After years of listening to every voice but Gods, I now know who I am. I am a fellow heir with Christ, a part of a royal priesthood. I am God's daughter, chosen to spend a lifetime and eternity with Him. It's not about fitting into a personality type or accomplishments and mistakes. It's about belonging to Christ. That is my identity.

If I feel condemned, it is not from God. God convicts, Satan condemns. You can tell the difference because conviction, from the Holy Spirit, motivates you to make changes and guilt, from Satan, paralyzes you.

It might be hard to forget the past, to ignore the words that have been beaten you're your head. The negative words and names wreak havoc on our souls! Sticks and stones may break my bones, but your words stick inside my mind for a lifetime. You see – the words do hurt. It's time for you to change your inner voice to one of faith, positivity and beauty.

Now that you've learned to identify it, let's move on to healing it, losing it, and sharing it with your children. After all, you are the one who has to teach them which voice to listen to. God has settled them in your hands, and that is a hefty fate.

CHALLENGE

Base your inner voice on the way that God sees you, not how you see you or how you think that the world sees you. No view matters but that of God. Where's your inner voice today? Is it based on God or others?

Heal It

I was successful. I didn't let my past do anything to me on the outside. I looked perfect. I worked for the number one accounting firm in the world. I got hired at the number one accounting firm in the world. Me—stupid me—I'm the one that was working there. I thought, *"Wow! I must not be stupid! How did I get a job here? Why did they hire me? I must be pretty smart."* That was the day it started to make sense to me like, *"Oh my word! Everything I've ever heard was just a big bag of lies."* It was only a bunch of trash trying to tear me down. You know what; maybe I need to stop hanging out with the trash.

> "The thief comes only to steal and kill and destroy; I have come that they may have life, and have it to the full."
>
> John 10:10

Jesus came to bring life and life abundantly, but I didn't know the difference because I wasn't taught the truth. I mean, I grew up in church, but my church taught me that I was going to hell. Every single week I went there, they were declaring, *"You're going to hell, you're going to hell."* They kept loading this stuff on me. They were trying to do was get me to receive salvation. But they never taught me that after I was saved, I became something really special to God, that I was healed and that my identity was formed through his eyes. I didn't know that after I was saved, I got a new identity, and I wasn't that old person anymore I thought I was. No one ever told me that. So maybe nobody ever told you that either. Right?

So there I was, Sheri Dawn, with the name that wasn't even mine, and I was this person that I thought I was in my own mind. I had been saved, but my identity was still Sheri, the rejected girl. The one who's daddy left. My Mom didn't even know I felt that way, but I felt abandoned and rejected by my dad. As I grew up, I got a new dad—one who would call me stupid and idiot and kick me until I felt nothing but worthless. My identity was shaping based on the things that were happening to me and the things that people were stating about me. I used to play softball and everyone on the team called me "motormouth". Yes, it was fitting because I never shut up. It was because no one would listen to me at home so I talked all the time. The identity of motormouth wasn't so bad, so I started to become a person that was known to talk too much. I was "motormouth". Outside, I portrayed that person while inside, I still felt like "dirty Sheri".

> *God is not your destination. He's your identity. He's your life.*

One day, when I started having some really positive inputs in my life, working in that amazing job and feeling not so stupid, I got a new identity. I started to be known as the hard worker. I started getting all these labels from people. People said things that made me feel good about myself so I took take that identity on. It became who I was. Sheri….she is a hard worker. That's my identity, I am a hard worker.

The truth is that the world will label us. People will label you and they will try to say so many things about who they think that you are. *"You are a good girl."* But good girl is not our identity; hard worker is not my identity. What I do is not who I am. Those things are completely separate. But as a society and in our nation, we see people's performance and we basically declare that their performance becomes their identity. If you are a professional football player, then that's who you are. What happens when you lose your career? You lose your identity. When people don't know who they are apart from what they do; when they lose what they did, then they, in essence, die!!! That's a mouthful. A motormouthfull.

So this was where my life took a turn. I headed down a path of destruction. I went so hardcore down the path of destruction that I didn't get up 'til I got in the gutter. When I hit the gutter I got up and said, *"All I know to do is run towards Jesus."* That's all I knew to do. I questioned God. Why? My life and what God has done in it—I don't even understand it. It's an incomprehensible love.

God has an order. He seeks us. He loves us. He's got an order and you know that he must because He created the world. I mean, think about how orderly it was on Day One.

When I look back at the little ten-year-old girl that was saved, I see now that I did

> *You are chosen, handpicked by the Father. Perfect. Healed. Whole.*

not really know God. God knows each and every one of us intimately. He knows every hair on our head, but I did not know Him. To me, at that time, God was like a life insurance policy; He kicked in at death. Seriously, at death, that's when God kicks in. That's all I knew, and I knew I didn't want to burn in Hell. I did not know Him.

> "FOR THIS REASON, EVER SINCE I HEARD ABOUT YOUR FAITH IN THE LORD JESUS AND YOUR LOVE FOR ALL GOD'S PEOPLE, I HAVE NOT STOPPED GIVING THANKS FOR YOU, REMEMBERING YOU IN MY PRAYERS. I KEEP ASKING THAT THE GOD OF OUR LORD JESUS CHRIST, THE GLORIOUS FATHER, MAY GIVE YOU THE SPIRIT OF WISDOM AND REVELATION, SO THAT YOU MAY KNOW HIM BETTER."
>
> **Ephesians 1:15-17**

God is not your destination. He's your identity. He's your life. He is your healer. He can help you heal it all. It's really hard to get your mind around what happens when you believe and confess the name of Jesus. It's hard to understand that His spirit comes in and dwells inside of us. *"What? I get the living God, the same spirit that Jesus had when He walked the earth that lives inside of me?"* It's Jesus's spirit that's deposited in me.

Because of His spirit, He declares we are masterpieces. We are chosen, handpicked by the Father. Perfect. Healed.

> "I PRAY THAT THE EYES OF YOUR HEART MAY BE ENLIGHTENED IN ORDER THAT YOU MAY KNOW THE HOPE TO WHICH HE HAS CALLED YOU, THE RICHES OF HIS GLORIOUS INHERITANCE IN HIS HOLY PEOPLE, AND HIS INCOMPARABLY GREAT POWER FOR US WHO BELIEVE. THAT POWER IS THE SAME AS THE MIGHTY STRENGTH HE EXERTED WHEN HE RAISED CHRIST FROM THE DEAD AND SEATED HIM AT HIS RIGHT HAND IN THE HEAVENLY REALMS, FAR ABOVE ALL RULE AND AUTHORITY, POWER AND DOMINION, AND EVERY NAME THAT IS INVOKED, NOT ONLY IN THE PRESENT AGE BUT ALSO IN THE ONE TO COME."
>
> **Ephesians 18-21**

That second part of the verse where it mentions that we may have the eyes of our heart flooded with so much light that we can truly know our inheritance in Him is amazing. But, for me, I could not grasp how I could be chosen: *"How could I possibly be a masterpiece? No one has ever truly shown me unconditional love. How could that be me?"* I really thought that God was sitting up on this big throne and He was mad at me. He was shakin' a stick and He was sayin', *"Look at your life. You caused that, first of all. Second of all, look at the path of destruction you left behind to all those people you burned."* That's what I thought God was, so I couldn't receive His truth. It took 16 years for God to get my attention, 16. I believed the lies that I was unworthy and insignificant.

> *You are not unworthy because it's Christ who makes you worthy in him.*

So, when I finally did turn around after 16 years of wandering like a nomad, searching for my missing piece, I would work so hard to try to improve myself and heal it. I would read all the self-help books there were, and I would come over here and I would look in the mirror and I would declare, *"You're a failure. You're stupid. You are insignificant. You are unworthy. You will never amount to anything. You're worthless. What can you do to cover yourself up? You could dress cuter. Ooh, you maybe could lose 15 pounds, get a new bra, do some better makeup, and get your hair fixed differently. You're still ugly. I hate you."* All I did, if you hear what I'm saying, all I said was my, me, I: *"I'm a failure. I'm horrible. My circumstances stink. I'm in so much pain."*

What I didn't know happened was that God had changed me from the inside. I didn't know that there was a glorious inheritance that didn't begin at death; that it began at life, the first day that I was really born again into His kingdom. Somehow I couldn't wrap my brain around that. I asked, *"You seriously live in me?"* You are in me. The most perfect sacrifice, my Savior. You chose me. You are my healer.

You are loved and You are chosen.

Suddenly I began to hear things like, *"I chose you. I have healed you."*

But I thought otherwise, *"No, you didn't. I can't be chosen. I'm not good enough."*

But when you can look at your reflection in a mirror and you can see Christ inside of yourself, that's the hope of glory. It's not anything I can do. It's not anything I can put on. It's not anything I can keep. I cannot do anything apart from Him. There's a song by Michael Jackson and they sang it the other night on American Idol. I'm going to sing it in a mirror. I'm not going to sing it, but here's what he said: *"I'm starting with the [woman] in the mirror. I'm asking [her] to change [her] ways. And the message, it couldn't have been any clearer. If you want to make the world a better place then take a look at yourself and make that change."* But this song is looking at the wrong image because if I look at myself I will never change the world, because it's Christ in me! That's the hope of glory, Christ in me.

In this mirror—this is a spiritual battle. This is a spiritual battle. We need weapons so we can battle, because I believe in my heart that I am not the only one that still to this day goes over here and says, *"Am I still okay? Hold on, let me check. Remember, you're still that girl, that little, tiny girl that was abused. Are you sure you're okay?"*

Sometimes I want to jump back into that old identity, but I have to run back over here and rely on Jesus who lives in me. As I rely on Him, as I focus on Him, what begins to happen is I become less. I don't have to battle this battle. I only have to focus on Him.

"HE MUST BECOME GREATER. I MUST BECOME LESS."
John 3:30

One of my deepest fears is that of rejection. I have had it since three years old. It became deeply seeded in me when my dad left. I am forty two, and it's been a progression of my entire life for he has kind of come in and come out; and come in and come out. He didn't talk to me all last fall. So it's a continual acceptance, rejection, acceptance, rejection. In the back of my mind, I really believe that every person will eventually reject me. It's like a deep seeded lie that was rooted by the enemy in me at a very young age. God is working that out and I know that I am accepted in Him but I still have that fear of rejection. So I assumed that everyone will eventually reject me. When that does happen, it makes my behavior engage loosely with people.

I know that I have lived my life in layers. I have worn on so many layers of protection to guard my heart because I have been hurt so much. Imagine that you are wearing a jacket. Now take it off. Unzip the deepest part of your soul shed it. You are going to think *"I change my mind. I don't know if I want to take off all my layers. I don't want anyone to know."* You'll go straight back to the battle.

Don't do it! I want you to dig deep. Is there some place in you that you've been like me and you've kept it locked up for a long time or it's still locked up today? Is there something inside of you that hasn't been repaired? For me, I lost my identity one night many years ago. I didn't know if I had a family or if I didn't have a family, but I did not feel safe in my own home ever again. I want to know: What's your story? Have you been wounded to the depths of your soul by someone? Have you been the one who wounded someone? Maybe you can relate with me to know what it feels like to feel rejected your entire life.

God started giving me his word and he gave me a hunger for it. I remember, a long time ago, I read my bible. I would look up verses on anger. It would read, *"Don't be angry."* I responded, *"Well that's helpful. Well that didn't help a stitch, I'm still angry. I'm still mad."* But then, all of a sudden I was actually serving in the church, and I typed the verses. I couldn't stop reading the bible. It became like living water and my soul was awakened. *"You mean I'm not stupid? Are you sure? Because I act stupid sometimes."* I realized, *"He told me stupid for so long—am I really not stupid?"* I realized that God has given me the mind of Christ and in Him I am not a stupid person. I'm not ugly because I am beautifully and wonderfully made in his image. I am not unworthy because it's Christ who makes me worthy in him. I'm loved and I'm chosen. How cool is that?

But God has chosen each and every one of us for a purpose. When you realize how much He loves you and He wants to know you, all of a sudden, you're able to take that trash in that landfill and start replacing it with truth. Then you put up a stop sign. A mom told me once that she taught her children to put up a stop sign. Stop it. Heal it. Stop thinking. Don't let the trash in anymore. I've got a stop sign up, and you'll hear me sometimes, going, *"Nope, I don't receive that. I already lived 26 of my years believing those lies and I refuse to live another day, I do not have enough life left to do that."*

So I've stopped allowing the trash in, and now I only let the word of God dump in. But to do that, you have to be in this. You have to know what this says because it's going to renovate all that trash—your marriage is going to get better, your finances are going to get better. I will tell you that I know this because of the truth of God *"Let God be true and every man a liar."* God's word is true and it works every time. It heals it every single time.

When I was wounded, that next day I got out of bed and I got dressed and I acted like nothing was ever wrong. There was a Band-Aid over the wound, but it wasn't healed. It was festering. I pretended for sixteen years.

I couldn't receive the truth. Believe me; I searched out every possible area to feel pleasant about myself.

> *"Too long I have lived in the shadows of shame*
> *Believing that there was no way I could change*
> *But the one who is making everything new*
> *Doesn't see me the way that I do,*
> *He doesn't see me the way that I do*
> *I am not who I was, I am being remade*
> *I am new"*
>
> by Jason Gray, Lyrics from I am New

CHALLENGE

How about you? Are you pretending or hiding in a swamp of shame? Do you protect yourself from others because you so desperately don't want to be marked by them?

Treasure It

I teach my kids about the significant changes that happen to people in the scriptures, for instance, Abram to Abraham. When they are changed by the power of God, when God comes in and wrecks their life, he changes their name. This happened a lot of times in scripture. This is why Abram is now Abraham and Simon was Peter. Simon meant pebble, but God said *"No, you are a rock"*. We need to understand that when we are born in Christ, when our kids accept Christ as their savior, we are a new person. Those people get a new name, and they were chosen, accepted. Their names might still be the same, but their identity is now in Christ.

> "THAT NOW WE ARE BORN OF GOD, WE ARE NO LONGER OF HUMAN DESCENT BUT NOW WE ARE BORN OF GOD, WE BECOME GOD'S CHILDREN".
>
> **John 1:12-13**

We know that born again doesn't mean to literally come out of the mother's womb again. It's about being born into the family of God so you have a new identity in Christ.

> "YOU WILL KNOW THE TRUTH AND THE TRUTH WILL SET YOU FREE".
>
> **John 8:32**

If we would teach our children when they are young what the truth is and what God says about them, they can have it anchored deep in their hearts. We need to treasure the gift of the word and remember the significance of what it claims. If I had been taught that, it would have saved me a lot of heartache. Before people start coming in and installing labels on our children, telling them who they are, how bad they are, how their performance defines them, make sure that they know what God says about them. Then they can be strong in the Lord throughout their adulthood because they can always go back to those foundational truths that we taught them. We need to teach them to treasure who they are by showing them that we treasure ourselves.

> "Therefore, if anyone is in Christ, the new creation has come: The old has gone, the new is here!"
>
> 1 Corinthians 5:17

In my family, we do a "leader of the day." I have children of different ages, and when they are three years old they get to participate in as the leader of the day. The leader learns to lead. Leading to us, is serving. The older kids learn to follow the younger kids; and the younger kids learn to follow the older kids. What we are really teaching them it is that you love your sister, your brother, in who God says they are. If you love them in truth then they are going to follow you, right?

We were driving past a farm the other day and this guy had a big sack of feed on his arm and all these cows were behind him, following him. We always follow the one who feeds us. Because we want to be fed, we are hungry. We are teaching our kids through our actions, to feed others in God's truth and they will follow you. If you are harsh and mean, ordering, "Get behind me," that's not actually being a leader. A leader is the servant. They are the feeder; my husband calls them *"feedership"*. "Stop saying, 'leadership,' it's *'feedership'*," he claims. Feed them and they will follow. They will learn to treasure what you have taught them.

When our kids know they are in Christ and they know they are loved and they know they are chosen, then they are not trying to elevate their selfish ambition to be noble. They will be rewarded based on their performances because they know they are good already and then they begin to love each other out of their overflow of the love of Christ in them. They begin to love each other in truth. You will hear my children assert, *"Don't say that about yourself. You are chosen. God loves you. He loves you so much."* They love each other in the truth.

So, in order to teach them to treasure themselves and each other, it starts with you learning to do the same. You've identified it, healed it, now start to treasure it! I took all that shame and that fear of rejection and being unlovable, not being good enough and poured it into my relationship with Christ. I took a long and winding road. I was after the treasure of having someone say that I was worthy enough; to have anybody love me, notice me. That was my treasure, and it was a long and winding road, almost 15, 16 years it took me to finally seek the high road. So, in my relationship with Christ, I had this huge wall that I had built that was rejection, shame: *"You're going to think that I'm not good enough, too, God. Will you reject me if I'm not good enough?"*

I was serving. I was the master at serving. If you want something done, call Sheri. *"I'm right here. Yes, I'll do it."* Because I need so desperately for those people to repeat, *"Sheri is wonderful. She's so brilliant. We love Sheri."*

I needed that to the bottom of my heart. I was seeking people's approval and not God's approval. I needed someone to treasure me. You see, faith comes from hearing. I heard all those words in my past. I heard, *"You're not good enough. You're stupid. You're rejected. You're not lovable. You're unworthy."* I not only heard them with my ears, I sang them out of my soul, I believed them, and I bought it. Man, I bought it. Even when I'd cross over into my relationship with Christ, nothing's different. *"What's wrong with me? There's no peace and joy. He said there was – I'm a new creation. I don't feel new."* I still felt like I was over there. What I learned was that I didn't really know God. I thought He was like my dad and my parents and all those people that had rejected me. I didn't know the truth. What I had to learn was that faith

> *We are a temple of the Holy Spirit. God's own Spirit comes in and makes His home in you. When you know what's inside of you, you can treasure it, it has value, and it should change you.*

comes from hearing. You will either be shaped by the world, which I did not want to be shaped by, or you will be shaped by the word of God.

If I told you that there was a treasure buried in your backyard, how many of you would go dig it up? What if that treasure was only a dollar? How many of you would go dig it up? No one. Right? But what if I told you that treasure was $10,000.00? Would you go dig it up? Who would go for ten? Ten? Quite a few, but not all of you. But what if I told you that treasure was $1 million? How many of you would dig it up? I would dig it up for $1 million with my bare hands.

The treasure is the better life that we have through the Holy Spirit. You need to have a revelation of that treasure. You have to know it. You need to know what you have. That will give you a hunger, a desire to chase after and pursue what has been given to you by God through the Holy Spirit. You're going to value it. You know, that treasure example is that if there's something that we value, we'll pour some effort into it, won't we?

Assurance says that when we believe on Christ, that cannot be stolen away from us. There is another piece to that puzzle that is completely awesome to me, and that is that we get a new life.

> "DO YOU NOT KNOW THAT YOUR BODY IS A TEMPLE OF THE HOLY SPIRIT WHO IS IN YOU, WHOM YOU RECEIVE FROM GOD?"
>
> 1 Corinthians 6:19

The Holy Spirit is in me? Is it possible that something can live in me? I looked up in the thesaurus all the synonyms for your temple. You know what your temple means? Your temple is a home. Your temple is a house of worship. Your temple is a house of prayer, and that's each one of us. Each one of us is a temple of the God that created the universe. We are a temple of the Holy Spirit. God's own Spirit comes in and makes His home in me. I can't get over that.

I lived in filth for so long and the fact that He would choose to live in me was unbelievable. *This dirty house.* It's like when your girlfriends come over, and you realize, *"Ohhhhh, my house is so filthy."* God's seen every corner, even those places where you have all of your stuff crammed in when your girlfriends come over. He knows because He lives, He dwells in you. When you're in the middle of your life, when you're in a crisis, and you're in a painful place, and we cry out, *"God, I don't feel You. Where are You? You're not here. I'm missing You."* He is still there.

I love Paul's prayer in Ephesians. He said, *"When you're in a place like that, you don't need more of God. You need more revelation of what you already have."*

For me, one thing that can change my behavior on a dime happened the first time I found out I was pregnant. I found out that I had a new life living inside of me and I immediately started to inventory: What medications have I taken? What liquid beverages have been in my body? What have I eaten, and how have I behaved? I immediately recognized that value of that new life. I knew then what I had, and it immediately changed my behavior. Some pregnant girls change their behavior. The other thing that women do when they're pregnant is they go out and they buy every single book on pregnancy as possible, don't they? *"What to expect? I want to know every single thing about this new life that is growing inside of me."*

When you know what's inside of you, you can treasure it. It has value, and it should change you. This is our treasure map. If you really went outside to dig for that treasure that I told you about – that $1 million – what is the first thing you would do? What's the first thing you would do? You would go get tools to dig it out with. You're probably not going to dig out with your claws and your little fingernails, right? You're going to get tools. The other thing you're going to do is you're going to ask, "Where is it? Where can I find the treasure that's buried in my backyard?" Probably, correct? You're not going to sit down and watch American Idol or your favorite TV show. You're not going to get on Facebook and tell all your friends. Well, some of you might tweet it, but you're going to immediately get out there and get your map and your tools, and you're going to get shovelling.

A pregnant woman—the first thing she does is go to the bookstore. We need to see that the Holy Spirit has tools that live in us, and this is our map to find it, and we need to go out and seek out what the tools are. We need to go to the bookstore. I think the Holy Spirit tools are like every man's dream garage. It's got every tool, every saw, everything you could possibly need to fix anything in your home. It's the chef's kitchen. It's got every stainless steel appliance that she could possibly dream of, every ingredient; every recipe book. It's got everything. The Holy Spirit has every tool that we could possibly need. Treasure the tools and use them!

For the sick, it's got the doctor that you need—the specialist that you need to help you get well. The Holy Spirit is a doctor with every tool we could possibly imagine, and the only way to find out what's in it is to open up the Bible. God has a better life for each one of us. He's got it. He's already designed it. He wants us to live out of the overflow of His Spirit in us, but we can't do it if we don't know that we have a treasure living inside of us. So today, you need to know that you have a treasure that is inside of you, and it is the Holy Spirit. It is God's Spirit, and you need to know it, so that you can go search out everything that He has and that is available to you, so that God can open up your eyes and reveal to you your calling, your inheritance, who you are in Christ, the power that's in and for you—the same power that raised Christ from the dead.

> "BUT VERY TRULY I TELL YOU, IT IS FOR YOUR GOOD THAT I AM GOING AWAY. UNLESS I GO AWAY, THE ADVOCATE WILL NOT COME TO YOU; BUT IF I GO, I WILL SEND HIM TO YOU"
>
> John 16:7

Now, I'm thinking, *"I've gotten to spend all this time with Jesus and sit at His feet and see Him teach and see Him heal people, and now He's not going to be here, and it's going to be better for me? I don't think so."*

So all of us, we didn't get to walk with Jesus, but sometimes I wonder what it'd be like to sit at His feet. I seriously thought that, *"I want to sit at Your feet. I want to see You raise someone from the dead."* But He declares in John, *"That's not profitable for you. That's not the best for you. That's not the better life. Here's the better life."* It's because when He died and left us, He left us with the Holy Spirit so that not only a few of us could be with Jesus, but that every one of us could experience Jesus in our spirits forever and ever. Every day, He is completely accessible to us. He treasures you.

He's not completely surrounded by the crowd where we can't get in. He's right here. He lives right here through the Holy Spirit, and you have to read your Bible and search out everything that belongs to you. Otherwise, there's going to be a treasure buried in your backyard, and you'll never find it. You'll never know the value you missed out on. You'll never know it.

I want to go through a few of these things that Jesus said the Holy Spirit is, and I'm going to go through a few, because this week in your homework, you've gotta dig. These are my revelations that God has given me, and He has revelations He wants to give you.

Why is it better to have the Holy Spirit than Jesus with you? It's better, because you always have a close friend. Wouldn't it be better when you feel lonely and sad and depressed to know beyond a shadow of a doubt that you have a friend with you at all times? There's never a minute that you're truly alone. Not in truth. You might feel alone, but that's you not living out of the truth. You're living out of your feelings. He's your counselor. Wouldn't it be better if you needed to have a conversation with someone, only to vent and get stuff off your chest, and you have a full-time counselor available that's not $100.00 an hour? He's free. He's your counselor. He's going to listen to you.

The Holy Spirit doesn't create tension in any friendship or any relationship with your spouse. He is available right there to counsel you all the time. When you're grieving or when you're mourning, when you're sad, He is your comforter. When I lost my mom, I thanked God every day because He comforted me. I had no words to pray, but the Holy Spirit held me tight, and He's that for you. It's inside of you.

> "PEACE I LEAVE WITH YOU; MY PEACE I GIVE YOU. I DO NOT GIVE TO YOU AS THE WORLD GIVES. DO NOT LET YOUR HEARTS BE TROUBLED AND DO NOT BE AFRAID."
> **John 14:27**

It's not peace, not peacetime, not wartime peacetime. It's a peace that you can be in the darkest time of your life and everyone else is looking in and asking, *"Why is she behaving like that?"* It is a peace that the world cannot understand. Isn't it a better life to know that you have that kind of peace through the Holy Spirit?

The Holy Spirit also will tell you, *"You have gifts you don't even know you have." You haven't even begun to tap into them."* He'll tell you that. *"I have so much that I want to give you through My Spirit."* I love this one for college students. Wouldn't this be a better life? The Holy Spirit will remind you of everything you've studied.

My daughter was saved when she was really little. She was eight years old when tested to be a memory master with her home school program. When she was finished we asked her, *"How did it go? Did you struggle with any points?"* She said, *"Mom and Dad, when I forgot, I prayed and asked the Holy Spirit to remind me, and He was faithful. He did everything."* Wow, why am I shocked by that?

One of the questions I get from people is, *"Sheri, how do I make this tangible for me? I mean is this really real? I see these things on the page. It says, 'The Holy Spirit's my comforter, my teacher, my reminder, my friend. He's my peace. He gives me all these fruits of the Spirit, but what does that mean in my life?'"* Personally, I remember a time in my life where I was angry and I was looking in the Bible. I'm angry, and the Bible would read, *"Do not be angry."* That didn't help me one bit, 'cause I'm so angry. I'm not supposed to be angry, but I'm angry. I don't know what to do about it, because it didn't make any sense to me. I was still treasuring my pain instead of treasuring God.

I want you to know that, today, I'm living proof. I don't know everything. I don't hit the mark all the time. I'm learning. The important part is to know what you have, to search it out, and to start. It's about moving forward. It's about attempting to know the truth. It's about seeking God and obtaining truth by picking up your map. It's simple. It's simple. It's so simple, but you know what? We have an enemy.

He wants to distract us. He wants to side-track us. He wants to keep our eyes on something else. We're too busy. We're busy with Facebook. We're busy with Twitter. We're busy with Biggest Loser and American Idol and all the other TV shows I don't even know that are on. Those are the ones I watch. I'm busy with some of the shows that I watch. I don't *not* watch TV, but what we've done is we make all those other things first, and seeking the truth, obtaining the truth is last.

This week, I spoke to a young girl who is in college. I asked her, *"Do you read the Bible? If you do, how much do you read the Bible?"* Then I asked, *"How much time do you spend on Facebook?"* The response I got choked me up, because she said, *"I spend an hour a day on Facebook and more than that on the weekends. I don't read my Bible because I don't have time. When I have picked up my Bible, Sheri, I don't understand it. I don't know what it means."* I'm afraid that we have a culture today where people start picking up their Bible and reading it, and the minute they don't understand it, they just throw their arms up. *"I don't get it. It's not applicable to my life. It's not. Let me go to Twitter and talk to people."*

I can tell you from my own personal experience, I grew up feeling abandoned, rejected, unloved, unworthy, and ashamed, and it produced fruit that was sin in my life. It simply did.

> "THIS IS WHY I BRING YOU THE SPIRIT. THIS IS WHY. I WANT YOU TO KNOW THAT I WILL NOT LEAVE YOU AS ORPHANS."
>
> **John 14:18**

"I will not leave you as an orphan, Sheri." "I will not leave you as an orphan, _____." Insert your name in the blank, because what He did was He deposited His Spirit inside of us as a deposit guaranteeing our salvation. He lives in us. That verse is in Ephesians 1:13-14. There is a better life. It's through living through the Holy Spirit. It's through knowing what you have. It's through searching it out and finding out what's available to you through the roadmap.

There is $1 million in your backyard, and if you found it, would it change your life? It would change mine. I wouldn't want to tell you what I would probably spend it on, but it would change mine, and that is the Holy Spirit that's inside of you. We're living in a culture that doesn't know what they have, and so they're living – we're living out of our feelings. We're easily offended. We don't have the joy that God intends for us to have, because we don't know what we have. Like Paul prayed, we need the eyes of our heart opened so we can know God better. So we can know our calling. So we can know our inheritance. So we can know the power that is in and for us. The same power that raised Christ from the dead. Treasure it!

Amazing, and that is what the Holy Spirit has for us. He's got the power that we need to share the Gospel. If you're afraid to share the Gospel, the power is in you. He's our strengthener when we feel weak. When we know that we can't do it on our own, He is that. Through the Holy Spirit, God has given us a full measure of Him, a full measure. God didn't give out portion sizes. There's one portion of the Holy Spirit, and everyone who's in Christ has the same portion. Billy Graham, same portion. Pastor Craig Groeschel, same portion. We have the same Holy Spirit, but, you see, we don't know what we have. So we're not being transformed by what's in us. It's not changing us and moving us.

One last thing, in order to treasure it, find your treasure and keep it safe, you've got to learn to recognize the voice of the Holy Spirit. There's your inner voice, and there's the Holy Spirit voice. Your inner voice is the voice that you hear when you're by yourself. When you're looking in the mirror, and you see yourself, what do you say? What do you say to yourself? I used to say things like, *"You're not good enough. You're not worthy."* The Holy Spirit's voice is so kind, and He's saying, *"I love you. I chose you. You're pure. You're holy. You're Mine. I bought you with a price, and you belong to Me. I adopted you. You're My child."*

When you listen to your inner voice, and you're in a sticky situation with a guy, you might say to yourself, *"I'm dirty. I'm shameful, and if I don't give myself to this man, he may leave me, and I'm afraid of that."* The fruit of those thoughts will be immorality. But if you know that you have the Holy Spirit in you, and you search out what belongs to you, and you know who you are because of that, you might respond this way. *"I am pure. I am holy. I am loved. I'll never be alone, and I don't have to give myself to this guy."* It is going to result in the fruit of self-control.

"I want to know You better, God. God, help each one of us get started on the journey. God, help us move forward, so we can have the eyes of our heart flooded, to know what belongs to us through Your Son, through Your Spirit, through Your life—the better life. I pray that You show us the power

that's in and for us, so that we can live out of it every day. Anyone that's hurting today, Father, I pray that You meet them as their Comforter, that You give peace to those that are wounded and hurt and in bad situations. Father, I pray that You flood the eyes of our heart and meet us where we are, God."

CHALLENGE

Do you know what you have? Are you ready to go out and search it out and find the treasure that God has for you? I hope that today you are empowered to go open up your map—your Bible—and know what the Holy Spirit has given you. I pray to God that you will hear His voice and learn to put it above your own inner voice.

Fight It!

One day I woke up and God showed me, *"You know what, Sheri? You didn't start off as a whole person in the first place. You started off like this."*

> "FOR ALL HAVE SINNED AND FALL SHORT OF THE GLORY OF GOD."
>
> **Romans 3:23**

All of us are broken, and we fall short of the glory of God. God showed me in His Scripture that He made me a new creation. Man, I love that verse because I was such a broken vessel, and so God took all the pieces of my life, and He placed them back together. I was restored.

But here's the problem. The problem is that far too many of us live out of this redeemed vessel. You see all these cracks? In my life, this is shame. This is the unforgiveness. I could not forgive myself for what I had done. No matter how much I'd healed it and I treasured it, the shame was still there, creeping up on me. These were like scars in my life that I carried. I bet you have some too—scars that you carry around. God showed me, *"Sheri, I didn't put the pieces of your life together like this. I brought it together like this. I didn't just put you back together. I made you a new creation."* He said, *"Sheri, you have failed to see yourself as a new creation that I have made you, and you have continued to see yourself in the flesh that you started as, with your brokenness just brought back together."*

Check this out. If this is our flesh, this is the war. It's time to fight. This is our flesh, and this is our spirit. When we live out of this view of ourselves, we see how fragile we are. We're fragile. These broken places, they are extremely tender. The fruit that comes out of living out of our flesh, our brokenness that we think has been restored and made whole, guess what it is? It's the fruit of being easily offended by your friends. When we live out of this flesh and our feelings, it's the fruit of being unforgiving, because we don't want to let anyone close enough to these wounds to even let them in anymore. As soon as you get close to a sore spot on someone who lives out of this, they withdraw every time.

The people that live out of this flesh, they live out of their feelings. They're living out of the flesh instead of the Spirit of God. There's no real hope for people who live out of this. When things are down, life is stale, or you lose a loved one or your husband leaves you or you lose a child or you scream at your kids or you strike out at a loved one, they crumble. They can't withstand it, because the fruit of the flesh is sin.

> *Until we know God and until we know who we are in Christ, how can we possibly begin to operate in the power that's in force?*

If we can know the fruit of our flesh and learn the fruit of living in the Spirit of God, then we can learn to identify our flesh from our spirit that is at war with one another. It's going to set us free. It's going to equip us to be able to engage in the battle, because I can stop myself and realize, "Ahhhhh, hold on. I'm living out of this vessel, because I've been offended by a friend, and I need to stop. This is the fruit of my flesh, and this is not the best. This is not what God had for me which is the best."

I believe what God wants us to do is that He wants us to take our flesh and give it to Him. Fight your flesh! Fight it! He covers every wrong. He covers every sin. He covers every broken heart, every tear you ever cried. He consumes it. We must become less and He must become more. When God looks at us, He never sees these cracks. He sees a perfect, complete child of His. He loves us. He loves us so much that He made us how we are instead of shabby. This is okay. It's complete, but it's not perfect.

I want to share with you a little story in Samuel 17 about a man named David. It's the story of David and Goliath. You have probably heard it before. I love David. I love his heart. I love his heart for the Lord. David was a shepherd, and he spent his time in the shepherd fields, and he took care of sheep. He was the youngest brother, and his brothers went off to war. His dad said, *"Okay, Son, go take your brothers some food, because you know you're too young to fight in the battle. You go take them some food, check on them, and let me know how they're doing."*

When David was there at the war field, he hears a Philistine come forward and roared, *"Who's going to fight me?"* And every single one of the army men ran in fear. They saw themselves through this old vessel, and they were afraid to lose their life to this Philistine. Every one of them ran off and hid, but David—he's standing there. He's thinking, *"Why is no one going to fight him?"* David decides, *"I'll fight him. I'll fight him,"* and, immediately, his older brother comes to him, and he immediately states, *"You're merely a shepherd boy, David. Why do you think you're going to fight him? You're the youngest in our family. You're only a kid. Why do you think you can fight him?"*

So, immediately, David's brother, who's living out of his flesh, becomes jealous. Maybe he was a little bit envious that his brother would have the courage to step up and speak, *"I'll fight him."* The first thing he does out of his flesh is he tries to take David back to his old identity before David was in the Lord. But you know what? David did not receive those messages his brother was sending him. Imagine if David had said, *"Ahhhhh, I am only a shepherd boy. I'm but a young kid. I'm the youngest of the family. There's no way I can do this. I won't do it. I quit,"* and went home. How would the story have ended if David had lived out of this?

Fight your flesh

But I love David's response. David did not live out of this. This is how we find victory to move from our flesh into the Spirit of God. We have to do what David did. We have to spend time with God daily, all the time, every day, every minute. That is what David did. Because he did that, he knew that he was tucked away in this God that he loved, that he sought time with every day; the

God that he prayed to, that he sang songs to, the God that was with him when he was all alone.

David goes and fights the Philistine. The Philistine comes forth, and the first thing he exclaims is, *"Am I a dog that you come at me with sticks, little boy?"* I mean can you imagine? *"Am I a dog, you come at me with a stick? Fetch. Come here, and I will give your flesh to the birds of the air and the beasts of the field."* Now, I don't know about you guys, but I might have ran.

But this was David's response. *"You come against me with sword and spear and javelin, but I come against you in the name of the Lord Almighty, the God of the armies of Israel."* He knew that he was one of God's chosen people. David knew he was God's. *"This day, the Lord will hand you over to me, and I will strike you down and cut off your head. Today, I will give your carcass of the Philistine army to the birds of the air and the beasts of this earth, and the whole world's going to know about it. All those who gather here will know that it is not by sword or spear that the Lord saves, but the battle is the Lord's, and He will give all of you into His hands."*

You see, I think the lesson we can learn from David is that David spent time with God. He surrendered his flesh to God and he knew God. He knew His character, and, secondly, he knew his identity in God. He knew he was the chosen, holy people of Israel. He never wavered. He never doubted. Think about that attack that's coming at you. You hear, *"I'm going to feed your flesh to the birds,"* and, *"No, I'm going to feed your flesh to the birds."* You have to know who you are to be a young little boy, go up against a nine-foot giant and know, beyond a shadow of a doubt, that you're going to win. That was David's confidence in the Lord. He had two things: a strong relationship with God and knowledge of who he was in God. He did not doubt it. His brother could not bring him down, and that giant Philistine could not steal away from him his identity in the Lord.

So we learn that we need those things to fight our flesh. That is the key to surrendering our flesh. While we're over here operating in our flesh and licking our wounds, what happens is David could've easily licked his wounds and gone home and left the battle. What happens when we're over here is we become selfish. We are utterly selfish. We can only feel for ourselves, and we're licking our wounds, and we feel this hurt spot. We're easily offended and easily hurt by friends and family. We are wounded. We're gentle little birds, and it's totally selfish. It's all about us. It's never about anyone else, because you can't even love yourself. Fight for it!

You must fight for your righteousness. Righteousness. This righteousness from God comes through faith in Jesus Christ. Let's talk about whoever is good by making cookies. We will say whoever has been well-behaved today gets a cookie or will get some desert or ice cream. If you have been really obedient, did your to-do list, got your stuff done, if you are good enough, you can get a cookie. We make lists like this for ourselves and for our children. They go, "Well, I got all my school work done. I turned in this and then I cleaned

> *Do not be conformed by this world. Be bold in Jesus. Fight for your identity.*

up my room and made my bed," and then we go, "Well but sorry that's not good enough." Can we keep saying that "That's not good enough; that's not enough?" We tried to find different ways to word it and then usually it's the smallest one that goes, *"I am good at Jesus."* You know, and we are like *"Yes. You get a cookie."* So we try to teach them that the goodness does not come from your works, ever. You can do good deeds but your goodness comes from Christ and Christ alone.

I want to give you three *reapons* for spiritual battle. They're ours; that's why I said *"reapons."* They're not weapons, they're *reapons*.

Rely on Jesus.

People always inquired, *"Sheri, how did God transform you?"* I have to rely on Jesus. I cannot rely on that self-reflection in the mirror at all, so I have to rely on Jesus.

Renew My Mind

I have to renew my mind every day, ladies. It's not like in the morning, get up, and have your quiet time. It is all day long. *"No, I'm not. I am a masterpiece. I don't care what you say. I'm not listening to you because you're the enemy and you want to distract me. This is a spiritual battle and I'm not going there."*

Resist the Enemy

That brings us to the third 'r' which is resist. We are women and the enemy is out to attack us. He wants our lives. He wants marriages. He wants the children. He wants the teenagers. He wants us all. He wants us reflecting on ourselves because when we reflect on ourselves we miss the power of Jesus Christ. You have got to resist your stinkin' thinkin'. We have to fight our stinkin' thinkin'.

Have you seen Google Earth? If you start out the big video, you can see the global perspective and realize, *"God is the god of all this."* But when you start zooming in to your insecurities, to what your husband did to make you mad, to how angry you are, how depressed you are, if you start focusing on *"I'm not going to be able to pay my bills next month"* instead of focusing on God, if you're focused on, *"I might lose my job. I'm scared because of these economic times. I might lose my job. I might not be able to pay the bills. I might not have a house. How will I feed my children? My marriage is destroyed. I don't even like my husband and I have to live with him,"* the more you inflate and you magnify those thoughts you get zoomed in and they become bigger than your God. I want you to know today that Jesus Christ's name is above every name. I don't care what your problem is, His name is above it.

Until we know God and until we know who we are in Christ, how can we possibly begin to operate in the power that's in force? You may have read that Scripture: *"I pray that they will know the unlimited, the unsurpassing, the greatness of the power that's in and for you."* It is meant for today, not at destination, not at arrival. It's for you. But until we get those things, there's an order to what God has. You have to know Him, you have to know who you are and then operate in the power. We will change the world by His spirit, by Him empowering us to fight.

CHALLENGE

I want to ask you: Have you been passive in the spiritual battle for your identity? Do not be conformed by this world. Be bold in Christ Jesus. Fight for your identity.

"Greater are you that is in me than he that is in the world. My words have the power of life and death. I do not allow words of death to be spoken out of my mouth.

Father, help me take possession of all your promises because you are worthy."

Reveal It!

There are traps out there—hidden little traps—waiting to drag you back to your self-deprecating view of you. They are there after you've healed and wait for the times when you are tired of fighting it. Then they appear. They come in many shapes and sizes.

One of the traps is that we compare, don't we? We compare and we judge, *"My kid is a year behind in math." "You're prettier than me. You're skinnier than me. I like your hair better than mine,"* right? *"Honey, kids, you're not leaving the house in those clothes because you're going to embarrass me,"* right? We're comparing constantly. We're constantly looking out, seeing mountains and circumstances so we try to change our behavior.

I asked some friends of mine, *"What is it that you look at and it automatically causes distress in your mind? What is that thing that it's like a trigger that comes up out of the blue?"* Like when our kids start to talk back and when our friends go out to coffee and they don't call and invite you. When I was young, I was left out all the time. I hate being left out. I hate being excluded. That is a trigger for me. You need to know what those triggers are, reveal them and reveal your own power!

But there are events that happen in our life. A friend of mine, back here at the table, she posted on out group meet, *"I'm two months behind in math and I'm thinking of sending my kids to public school."* Who told her that? Who told her kids are two months behind in math? Who cares? You know what? Maybe your kid isn't going to be a mathematician or a CPA. First Corinthians 1:25 informs, *"The weakest things of God are stronger than the strongest things of man and the wisest things in man."* Okay? So who told us that? You know, in Genesis 3, when Adam, after eating the apple, went and hid. God inquired, *"Why are you hiding?"* Adam is all, *"Because I'm naked?"* I would hide too. God said, *"Who told you that?"* Who told you your kids are behind? Who told you that you aren't doing well?

We have sicknesses come up on us. We have trials come. We may not be able to make the bills. You may be praying right now that God would give you the finances that your family needs. You may actually lay pressure on your husband to bring home more money so that you guys can do all the things that you want to do. Or maybe your husband is out of work right now. We constantly have trials—you know why? John 16:33 reveals, *"In this world, you will have trouble."* I mean, that's pretty clear. We're all going to have troubles. Reveal them and reveal God!

> *We live in a broken, fallen world so we constantly have trials, but Jesus Christ came so that we could live abundantly. Settle for nothing less.*

Here's why. We live in a broken, fallen world. You know that. But the devil wants to come and steal, kill and destroy. In John 10:10, in the Rastafarian version, it reads, *"Da steala guy, he ony come fo steal, kill, an bus up da place. But I wen come so da peopo can come alive inside, an live to da max."*

Jesus Christ came so that we could live abundantly. Abundantly. I don't know about you but every single day, I have the opportunity to live with the stealer and the killer and the destroyer. In a moment, he can take out my kids. My kids call me strict with a whole lot of fun. Every single day when they fall out of line, we have an opportunity to either build them up or tear them down. When we tear them down, we're submitting to the stealer, did you know that? When you tear your kids down, when you raise your voice at them, when you choose to walk in your flesh, you're tearing them down. But, when you pause, and you declare, *"Nu uh, this is the stealer, I see your fingerprints."* Jesus Christ came to bring life and life abundantly.

We need to reveal our triggers. What are those? I am the queen of triggers. John 14:27 reads, *"Do not let your hearts be troubled."* That word, troubled, in the Greek means to stir or to agitate it. Who has pet peeves?

Oh, I have so many pet peeves. What is that? That's an agitation, right? When we hear pet peeves—one of mine is smacking—we move away from it. So we need to reveal our triggers. What are the things that when we're abiding in the spirit of God, we're experiencing the fullness of his joy, and we go off like, *"Oh, in the presence of the Lord is the fullness of Joy. What was that? Was that smacking? I think I heard smacking. I'm pretty sure that was smacking. Who's smacking?"* We've got a smacking signal in our house because it bothers me that bad. What are our triggers that pull us out of that abiding in our Lord, abiding by the spirit? What are they? We all have them.

Because I was abused when I was a child, one of my big triggers is being touched in the middle of the night. It's a huge trigger. When that happens, it triggers me into my flesh, into my emotions. I become touchy and frustrated. I've got to be quick to identify that trigger and voice "That's a trigger," and surrender it to God.

Hebrews 12 mentions that we need to throw of everything that hinders us. Every agitation and every pet peeve we have—it's a hindrance to dwelling in the fullness of the Lord. We've got the fullness in us. Remember that? It's already here, but we are the ones, ourselves, our old habits, biding in our worldly emotions that keep us from experiencing the fullness every day. The four R's of more will reveal exactly what you need to do overcome those triggers. It's pretty crazy that revealing something negative actually reveals something positive!

The first R of more is revelation. Revelation – we all need revelation of God to know Him better. We need the eyes of our heart flooded so that we can know the truth. We need an eye-opening experience, a revelation, to see the things of God that we cannot possibly see with our physical eyes. Paul, when he is on the road to Damascus, he was blinded by a light. That light blinded him physically, but God gave him spiritual sight after that happened. We all need a revelation. I believe that God wants to give it to us because He's poured it out in His Scripture, and He's made it clear that He wants us to have that more. He wants us to have that revelation. I want revelation. What we have to do is ask for it. He is faithful. When we ask, He provides. He gives every time. He is so faithful.

Renew. The second R of more is to renew. Renew, as defined in the dictionary, is to make new or to make like new. I like the word renovate. It makes me think about some friends of mine. They bought a crack house. It's huge—4400 square feet—a ton of people lived in it. It was an amazing house. My husband and I and a whole team of our friends went over to help them clean up and get this house renovated. It was hard work to renovate that house. It was hard work just to go into it. There were cockroaches the size of your hand. It was completely disgusting. I'm still having nightmares about those cockroaches to this day. There were actually needles inside of fast food containers in the top of closets where these people had been. So we went in, and cleaned up all the trash. We began to make this old property new. We renovated it. We renewed it.

The Bible, in Romans 12:2, it suggests, *"Be transformed by the renewing of your mind."* Renovating a home, it's hard work. It's hard. I'll tell you, it took a lot of time, a ton of weekends for our friends to do this together. Well, renovating your mind is the same way. It takes time. Things that you didn't anticipate are revealed. You find holes in the walls that were hidden or pipes that were broken below the surface. It takes commitment. It takes courage to choose something different than what everyone is choosing.

What I've found in the battle for renewing my mind with the truth in God's Word is that I'm met with resistance. When I think of resistance, I think of weight training. A resistance is any force that opposes movement. Every time we get ready to do something new, there's this force that comes against us that it's resistance. It keeps us and holds us back and kinda holds us there. It's some pressure. It's like weightlifting. I go to pick up a weight, and I have to work really hard to get it picked up. It is a whole lot easier to never pick up a weight and do resistance training than it is to pick up the weights and do the work.

I want to share with you a verse from Mark 4. Pretty much the whole chapter is about the parable of the sower. The farmer goes out, and he sows seed into the ground. He sows seed in good quality soil. Then he gets a harvest. He's sown his seed, and, as he waits, he eventually gets a fruit or a tree or whatever he's planted. There's actually a harvest there. The Word in Mark 4 actually reveal that some of the farmers, they either reap 30-fold, 60-fold, or 100-fold. What I think is completely amazing about this verse is a verse I had never read before until this year. It is Mark 4:24. It tells us the key to know whether or not you can reap the 30, the 60, or the 100. How did some people reap 30? How did some people reap 100? I want to reap 100.

I don't know about you, but I want to reap fruit from God's Word being planted in my life. I want to reap abundant fruit in my life. In Mark 4:24, it reads, *"Be careful what you are hearing, because the measure of thought and study that you give to the truth you hear will be the measure that comes back to you."* He gave us the secret, an insight into the mystery of how to have fruit in your life. How can I have more spiritual transformation? How can I have more revelation from God? I get my mind renewed when I dwell on God's Word. The more I dwell on it, the measure that I place into it is the measure that I get back. So if I'm only going to church one hour a week, and that's the measure that I placed into it, that's what I'm going to get back.

Do you want more? If you want more, you have to be willing to invest in it. Resist resistance. Declare, *"I'm not going to let the hard work go undone. I'm going to do the hard things. I'm going to make different choices. I am going to renew my mind with God's Truth."* That's the only way. He gives us the key. Believe that the Word of God is God-breathed and He actually said it. You will do what it says if you know Him and if you love Him. When you know God and you love Him out of the overflow out of your heart, you read these words say, *"Be careful what you're hearing."*

If I watch TV and movies and play video games and put all that stuff in me, and then I set one hour of God in my life a week, what do you think my return is going to be? It's not going to be a fruitful life in Christ. It's not going to be a fruitful mind renewed that gets more. You've seen that one person before, where you've said, *"I want what she has."* But maybe you only want the easy way, like a diet pill. Something that you take for a short period of time, and it gets you results. There is not an easy way. There's not a microwave ability to get truth in your life. It takes work.

Rely. So we've talked about two R's: revelation, and renewing or renovating your mind. The third R is to rely. Rely as you're renewing your mind. Let's go back to the house. When we renovated this house, you did it. You saw the old home, and now you see the new, and you helped do it. Guess what? You know where all the flaws are. You know where every little bit of paint got on the corner, and you didn't clean it up. You know where those cockroaches used to live, and still don't go to that corner. You know those things. You know them because you've seen them. You saw the old, and now you have the new. So you have to choose every day to not look back at the old, to not look at the former things. (read Isaiah 43:18-19).

You know what that verse tells me? It is that when we're looking back, we can't reveal what God is doing because we're so focused on our flaws and what we've done wrong. I purposely will tell you guys that I have not lived a clean life. I had a hard life. I made really poor choices. I am a sinner who has sinned more than it's imaginable, and it makes me thank God so much for His Grace that He's given to me, but it's so easy. It would be so easy to turn around and look back at my past and cry, *"You're not worthy. You weren't chosen to do this."*

Have you seen the old? You remember where you've been and what your footprints looked like. It's so easy to look back, but when I do that, I can't see God, and I can't reveal what He's doing today. You know, today, because my mind is renewed,

We all need a mental renovation.

because I've done the hard work for years, I've been lifting God's Word. Every day I choose. I lift it. I breathe it. I meditate on it. I pray in the car. I crave God's Word. That's our desire for you – that you will crave God's Word, because, as you make those hard choices and God renews your mind, the enemy comes up behind me and tries to steal, kill, and destroy me. The enemy suggests, *"Look at your past, honey."* If I'm even tempted to turn over my shoulder, I respond, *"No. No, I've been bought with a price. Jesus Christ took all of that, and He alone makes me worthy. You shush. Get behind me, Satan."* I say that. We need to say that. We've gotta learn to rely on God and look forward and stop looking at the flaws and looking at the past.

So let's review. The first R is revelation. We all need revelation. It doesn't ever stop. I get revelation every day. The second one is renew or renovate your mind. The third one is to rely on God. Rely on the truth, and then the fourth one is resist. When you know what you have in Christ, and you know who you are in Him, you will begin to set up barriers for the enemy.

The crack house that my friends that renovated—after they got it all done, the house was a valuable piece of property. Underneath the dingy carpets, gorgeous hardwood was revealed. It was amazing. It was a really outstanding house. The first thing they did when they finished – because they recognized the value – is they prop up a huge 10-15-foot fence around their entire property. They recognized, *"What I've renovated now has value, and I'm going to do everything in my power to protect it."* As believers, when our minds are renewed, when we're relying on God, we've got to start resisting the enemy with installing barriers around us.

Be careful what you hear, and you'll start to see things in your life, and you'll acknowledge, *"Because God has given me this truth, and I've renewed my mind, and I know the truth, all of a sudden, those things I used to do, they don't seem okay anymore."* They're not. It's not okay. I mean this is my personal preference. I don't judge you, but it's not okay for my family to watch rated R movies anymore. We don't even watch PG-13 if there's too much content that we don't agree with, because we are guarding our mind every day.

> *When you know your identity in Christ and WHAT you have in Him, you will truly begin to resist the enemy because you are no longer deceived by him. You realize he is powerless over you.*

With several of my friends, I have seen marriages crumble because of inappropriate relationships discovered through social media. To resist the enemy, my husband and I have controls over our computers, phones, and social media accounts. We share passwords. We share everything.

When you're relying on God and resisting the enemy; you will still be met with a strong force against you. Hold fast to this unbelievably incredible verse in Jeremiah 23:29 – *"Is not My Word like a fire, like a hammer that breaks in pieces the rock of the most stubborn resistance?"*

So if you can take these four R's to stand against resistance. It's simple. Where there is truth is, there is freedom. I've never been more free! Evaluate yourself deeply. Are you receiving daily revelation from God or do you need revelation from God? If you need it, ask Him. Pray Ephesians 1:17-20 over yourself. I have prayed this daily for eleven years, and it has changed me. I hear from God constantly. I can quickly discern Him from my inner thoughts. The Bible is more clear and simple than it's ever been. His love is so simple and pure. His vision for me is clear. His relationship with me is intimate. My identity is rooted in His love.

Do you need your mind renovated? If so, just do it. Commit today. Set aside a time to read the word and commit it to memory. Pick up the sword, the Word of God. Pick it up and get into it. Commit to it today. No longer allow the enemy's resistance to defeat you.

Do you need rely on God more? Identify your worries. Pray over them. Now, write down your concerns and anxieties. Secure them in a box as an offering surrendering them fully to God. Stop looking backward at your past – sins, hurts, and offenses. Start looking forward by imagining what God can do in and through your unoffendable heart!

Do you need to resist the enemy? Is there a place right now where the enemy is involved in your life? Prop up your barriers. Proclaim now, *"No more. I resist in Jesus name! The enemy has no power over the living God!"* No more. Stop tolerating defeat, sin, strife, and offenses!

I believe there is a cycle. God reveals revelation. We renew our mind. We choose to rely on Him. We resist the enemy when the enemy attempts to steal our Words from God! Repeat – He provides new revelation, etc. I am sure you have met people that seems so mature in their walk with God…right?! You know the ones that you want to throat punch because you feel like a baby around them? Inwardly, youre jealous because you have known God longer, but feel like you still know nothing. Why is it? Because theyre hungry. They listen – Obey God – renew their minds – resist the devil and continue going deeper and deeper into His heart.

This is how we can obtain more revelation! Process through all four steps so that the next revelation will come. Don't squash the voice of God by ignoring Him when He speaks to you! When we surrender to His voice, the revelation never stops. It is an endless cycle.

How big can our revelation of God grow? Continue asking for more revelation, renew your mind, stop resisting truth, and do the hard work of resisting the devil, decept, and offense.

CHALLENGE

Find someone to share this with: Confess, *"Here's where I am. Here's what I need."* And then make a commitment. Make a commitment to not let resistance defeat you anymore. Reveal it!

"A PEACEFUL HEART LEADS TO A HEALTHY BODY; JEALOUSY IS LIKE CANCER IN THE BONES."

Proverbs 14:30

Believe It!

Here's the problem. I look around believers, and we are so sad. We're oppressed. We're down, depressed. We do not know this truth. We might have head knowledge of it, but we don't believe it. We don't believe it in our hearts. We don't live out of it, and we don't act out of it. Listen to this. I want you to hear this again because it is powerful. *"I have given you authority and power and physical and mental strength and ability over all the power the enemy possesses."* The enemy has nothing on you. Are you in God? If you're born again, and you're in Him, and you're a son or a daughter of the Living God, nothing can harm you in any way.

That does not mean you won't have trials and things that you go through, but it does mean you don't lay back and whine and moan like the rest of the world and think that you're helpless. You're only a prey. The Bible says that the enemy roams around like the roaring lion. He's not the lion. Jesus is the Lion and the Lamb. We've got to stop being blinded by the lies of the enemy, that he's trying to come in and pretend and wear us out. We have to stand firm on this verse that declares, *"Over all the power that the enemy has,"* and not give him any glory, any honor, and know that we know our birthright is that nothing will harm us in any way.

In Ephesians 6, in the armor of God, it actually mentions that there is the helmet of salvation. With the helmet of salvation, even in death nothing will harm us in any way, because, remember, we already died in this life. I think we miss that. I don't think we know that we died to our bloodline when we received Christ, and, today, we're alive to God. We are already seated in eternity with God. That's a new view of God that we haven't seen. We're already seated with Him. So when we die to this physical shell, it's no big deal. We're already there. We only have to believe it!

Our Father's name is Abba, Father. It's on our birth certificate. We've talked about what our birthright is, but with rights come responsibilities. Every birthday of our kids, we sit down and we make a list of new rights that they get, like new privileges. What new privileges should they get since they've increased in age? And then we sit down, and say, *"Now, if we gave you privileges, you'd probably be a spoiled brat. So, now, you're older. We need to increase your responsibility."* So, with each birthday comes a new responsibility.

When I had my daughter, I did not know what to do with her. She was dependent on me. I had never been around children, and I had to be with her all the time. I thought I had to sit beside her and sleep beside her, and I had to feed her every meal. I fed her every two-and-a-half hours for the first eight weeks it seems like. I took complete care of her. Without me, she would have died. Then she got older, and she started feeding herself those little Cheerios and all those little snacks. Then one day she started walking, and she would fall down, and so there I am again. I was her little protecting arm everywhere that she went. She believed that I could do anything to protect her.

> *Today is the day that you have to stop living on someone else's view of God. You have to get your view from God Himself.*

But now, we'd look at our have three girls – and this last vacation, we realized we've hit a new stage in raising our kids. All of a sudden, they all packed themselves. Everyone dressed themselves. Everyone repacked themselves. They did absolutely everything. It required virtually no management from me. When we're born again in the Kingdom of God, there is a season of that same intimacy, like you would take care of an infant child. There's that stage where you need to be nurtured and be under someone that's caring for you, feeding you, telling you, "Here, read this Scripture. Here's what this means." You've got that stage.

God wants you to sit at His feet. He's the author of your adoption manual. The way to know what belongs to you and what your responsibilities are is to ask Him. Spend time with Him. Then you've got the next stage, which is where you've got this Word, and you start getting hungry, and you start to fall in love with God. All of a sudden, you notice that this adoption manual says that you might need to change a few things in your life that you've been doing in the past that don't necessarily make God very happy. So now you need to make some changes. That walking stage, when our kids are learning to walk, and they're toddling, they're doing that on faith. They think, *"I stood up. I'm going to try to go somewhere."* It's so cool.

Well, that's what we have to do in the next stage. We have to learn to start walking, and say, *"Okay, God, You said so. It looks like I can do this, and I'm going to start doing this."* A friend of mine's father said, *"Obedience brings understanding."* So there's a stage where we need to start learning, obeying or doing it because we've read it, and we know it, we believe it and trust that as we start taking those steps, it'll bring understanding.

There's a third and final step where we all are in believing it, and that's the adult stage. It's an adult step. It's where you've learned, and you know beyond every ounce of knowledge you've ever known in your life. It's the wisest thing ever. You know that you know that you know this Scripture that I gave in Luke 10:19, that the enemy has no power over me. You know it in your heart so deep that you become an adult, a spiritual, mature Christian.

When things come your way and trials come up, your response is actually different than the way someone who's lost or of the world might be, or maybe as an infant Christian. When you're a spiritual adult, and you're growing, and you're maturing, you know that you know, *"My God protects me."* Remember, one of our birthrights is we're protected. When you know that from the top of your head to the bottom of your toes, you become a strong oak of righteousness. Don't solely say it. Believe it.

I love the Scripture where it says that a tiny, little mustard seed actually can grow so big that its branches become so big that a bird can actually make its nest in it. In 1 Corinthians 3:1-3, Paul said this, and I love it. It reads, *"Brethren, I could not talk to you as spiritual men, mature spiritual men and women of God. I couldn't talk to you that way. You know why? Because you're not spiritual. You're still a man or a woman in the flesh in whom your carnal nature dominates you."* Your carnal nature is your natural nature.

"As mere infants in your new life, unable to talk yet. I fed you with milk, not solid food, for you were not strong enough yet. You were not ready for it. Even still, you're not strong enough to be ready for it. For you're still unspiritual." This is time later. In the beginning, he declared, *"I can't talk to you about spiritual things, but all this time has passed, and guess what? I still cannot talk to you. You're still unspiritual. You have the flesh that's under control of ordinary impulses. For as long as there's envy and jealousy and wrangling and fractions among you, you're unspiritual. You're of the flesh, behaving after a human standard like unchanged men."*

He's talking to people that should be mature adults by now, and they're not. I can't imagine how that breaks the heart of God. You don't have to walk with God for 20 years to be a mature Christian. I've seen people grow up into mature Christian in two years. What changes it, what causes you to grow up is the time you spend with God in getting your view of Him. You believe in him. Wear your spiritual goggles and get your view lined out, because you have a personal relationship with Him. Then you have to look at your adoption manual every day, all the time. Long for it. Linger for it more than you do any technology: e mail, Twitter, Facebook. I don't know. Whatever it is that's out there. This is the most important instruction that you have.

Today is the day that you have to stop living on someone else's view of God. You cannot go to church and get that view of God. You have to get your view from God Himself. He's willing, and He's able. You have to believe it! It's time for the church to grow up and stop living on spiritual milk. God wants you to grow up. He wants you to know that your birth certificate says Abba Father, so you can cry out to Him. He wants you to know your birthright; that there's this amazing Protector and Lover of your soul; that longs for you, and longs to know you. He wants you to be responsible so that you don't waste the grace and the blood of Jesus Christ that was spilled out for you, and do nothing. You'll never achieve your calling in this life if you don't grow up and start believing in who you are.

There is a verse in scripture that is always used for one purpose. It's the parable of the lost coin. It's really about salvation. It's about one person who comes to Christ and heaven rejoices. But one time, I read this verse and God used it to speak to me. I want to share the verse with you. The parable of the lost coin is this: suppose a woman has ten silver coins and she loses one, doesn't she light a lamp, sweep the house and carefully search until she finds it? When she finds it, she calls her friends, her neighbors and together they rejoice. *"Rejoice with me, I found the lost coin!"* When I heard that verse, the lord spoke to me, He said, *"Your child is a treasure."*

I want you to know that your child is a treasure. Inside of them are little lies and they are like lost coins. They're little lies that the enemy has planted in them that will cause them to doubt themselves, to doubt who I am, to walk away from me. They're little lies. Your job as their mother is to search for every single lost coin or every single lie they believe. Search the corners of their heart so that the truth of God can get in those places and set them free. Do you want that for your children?

I don't know if you grew up like me, but it took me my whole life to realize that the whole time I believed a bunch of lies. A lie believed as truth will affect you as if it's true even though it's not. But as God's children, the only thing that we should believe as truth is God's word.

"Let God be true and every man a liar."

Romans 3:4

This includes your own man—yourself, your inner voice that talks to you. You know that voice? I can look and the mirror and think, *"You're so ugly."* When I wake up in the morning, my hair is like this, and I think, *"How do people even recognize me when I look like that? Do I look that ugly all of the time,"* right? Do you ever believe those lies about yourself? Yes? Who hasn't?

How do you start believing when you are faced with lies all of the time? How do you find the truth? I'm going to go through what are some signs are that would reveal to you whether you or your children believe a lie. One is emotional outbursts. I want to reiterate something before we move on. If we have an enemy that wants to steal, kill and destroy, we can't see that enemy. If we don't use our lie spy equipment and really dig into the hearts of our children, it is no different than opening the front door at night and letting any intruder have access to your home and to your family. That is how important it is that we learn to identify lies in ourselves, because if you can't identify it in you, you won't be able to identify in your kids.

Back to the emotional outburst. God created emotions. Our emotions are indicators. They're like lights on the dashboard of your car. The car company didn't come up with the engine lights to make you mad and think, *"How much is this going to cost me?"* They did it to warn you and tell you, *"Hey there's a problem under the hood."* And that's what emotions are. They're indicator lights to show us that we need to do a heart check. Why am I emotional about something? Because at the root of that is a lie believed. The only way to resolve that is to dig in deep to your kids. Self-deprecating comments cause those emotional outbursts. My kids say that I'm the queen of self-deprecating comments. Do you ever say anything negative about yourself, such as, *"Oh my hips are too big,"* or, *"I still have this mom's belly." "Does it matter how many half marathons I run?"* The problem is that at the root of that comment is a lie believed that *"I'm not good enough. That the heart in me isn't good enough,"* right? The world is trying to get our girls and our boys to believe that lie. The world will plant a lie in their mind that makes them think, *"I have to look a certain way to be beautiful, to be accepted."* So when we see those self-deprecating comments, we know that there's a lie at the root of that.

Do you believe your lies or His truth?

Another lie is criticism of others. And we know critical people—when you're critical of other people, we know the root of that is that, *"I feel really bad about myself so if I can find the faults in someone else, then it's going to make me feel better about me,"* right? But we've got to know who we are in Christ so that we can love others no matter what.

Another lie is lack of motivation. I love this one because we've got a generation with a lack of motivation. But there's a root at that. What is the root? The root is that they don't know that God created them for noble works.

> "FOR WE ARE GOD'S HANDIWORK, CREATED IN CHRIST JESUS TO DO GOOD WORKS, WHICH GOD PREPARED IN ADVANCE FOR US TO DO."
>
> **Ephesians 2:10.**

Another lie is disobedience. Another sign that someone believes in lies is disobedience.

> "IF YOU LOVE ME, YOU'LL OBEY MY COMMANDMENTS."
> John 14:15

Disobedience of any child is a direct result of their heart. It's a relational issue. It's a relationship issue.

Another lie is rebellion. When we see kids being rebellious, there's a lie believed in that. Let me go through these a little bit faster. They follow the crowd and they don't have the strength to stand up to peer pressure because they aren't confident in who they are. They're not confident being alone. They'd rather have friends that are bad than friends that are upright.

Another lie is fear. I have a daughter, and she went through 39 days of horrific fear. My family—we prayed for her and prayed for her. The root of that is that we don't really understand that God has redeemed us. He is our safety net. We've got the helmet of salvation. Even in death, we're still fine. So there's a lie believed at the root of fear.

Quitting. Anybody ever quit before? I say I'm a runner because I've spent my life running. When I thought I would fail at something, I would quit before it would fail on me. You've ever done that before? Ran away? Well, there's a lie believed in that—that if I fail, it steals away from who I am.

Strife. In my family, we have a zero tolerance for strife. Somebody asked me, *"How do you do that? How do you have a zero tolerance?"* It's simple. It's not tolerated. In James 3:16 it explains that strife is an open door to chaos and every evil work. Strife is selfish, right? Strife is always caused from *"I want my way yesterday."* So when you're fighting with your spouse, you've got to look inward and realize, *"Man, I believe a lie that I have to have my needs met by my spouse or by this. I've got to be right."*

Another lie is the inability to sit still. How many of you have seen children that can't sit still for five minutes? We know that in Christ, in our rest is when we renew our strength, Isaiah says. So there's a lie that believed that I need to be entertained. *"Entertain me! What's next? I'm bored! Help me not sit still."* We've got to train our children to identify those lies.

So those are some of the attributes we'll see in ourselves. Do you recognize yourself in any of those? I've kind of had this zero tolerance to lies. If you came up to me and said, *"I believe you believe in a lie about this,"* I would sincerely listen to you because I want to know. I don't want to be listening to the father of lies. He's the father of lies.

> "THE SPIRIT OF THE SOVEREIGN LORD IS ON ME, BECAUSE THE LORD HAS ANOINTED ME TO PROCLAIM GOOD NEWS TO THE POOR. HE HAS SENT ME TO BIND UP THE BROKENHEARTED, TO PROCLAIM FREEDOM FOR THE CAPTIVES AND RELEASE FROM DARKNESS FOR THE PRISONERS."
>
> Isaiah 61:1

Are you poor? Jesus has good news, right? This is life abundantly. It's the good news. He's set me to bind up the broken hearted. Somebody in here is broken hearted. We lose loved ones every day, don't we? Who's broken hearted? God sent Jesus to bind up your broken heart. It's finished. He did it on the cross. He came to proclaim freedom. Are you in bondage to your flesh? Are you in bondage to your own temper tantrums? Jesus came to proclaim freedom for the captives. He came to release us from darkness.

Wow. Do you ever feel down and discouraged and depressed and you literally want to move to China? You've started packing your bag and I don't even want to go to China. But it sounds better sometimes, right? We don't have to go to China, we can run to this. Run to Jesus. Believe in Him. He's not a word. He's not just somebody we just worship. He's somebody we know intimately, more intimately than you can know a man. Because he lives in you, there's no one that can come closer. He came to comfort all who mourn. In tsunamis you find out who the comforter is, right? Or do you grieve like the rest of the world?

I was just mentioning other day, *"Jesus, why don't people see it? They need it, they're so desperate. I see it everywhere. Everywhere I go, I see hurt, wound, discouragement and depression and I can't take it."* There's a fire shot up in my bones and it wants to get out and proclaim the name of Jesus Christ and his freedom. He's already brought it, and he's already delivered it. It's available to everyone. No exceptions. He has no respect over persons and he doesn't have favorites. I felt like he said, *"Christians aren't any different than the rest of the world. We are not supposed to grieve like the rest of the world. We're not supposed to fight like the rest of the world. We're not supposed to live in bondage, because we've already been set free."* Freedom is here. We're the spirit of the Lord. There is freedom. Is the spirit of the Lord in you? Do you believe it?

You don't have to beg God for freedom. If you're begging God for freedom, He is saying you're not getting it. He is answering, *"I already gave it to you. Honey, step into it. Today, you have before you life and death, blessings and curses, today choose life. Choose the abundant life."* Sheri chose the abundant life today. He came to bestow on them the crown of beauty instead of ashes, oil of gladness instead of mourning, the garment of praise instead of a spirit of despair. Instead of moaning and pity partying and whining when you're in despair, pick up some praise. Seven minutes worth of an awesome song and you're not going to remember what you're upset about—especially when you're older. The older you get, the more you're think, *"What was I doing? Could somebody tell me what I was doing? I don't know."*

And listen to this. Here's the deal. We will be called oak of righteousness. It will be our reputation. Our reputation is oak of righteousness—a planting of the Lord on display for His splendor, for His glory. That's what happens when we step into the abundant life of Jesus Christ. Once you get it you will renew. You will restore the places that have been devastated. You will renew cities, homes. You will renew your home. The joy of the Lord will renew your home. When you step into freedom, your husband will be wonder, *"What happened? Where did my old wife go? For some reason, you don't worry like you used to. You're not concerned about your financial peace. You're at peace. You're letting me make the decisions? What happened?"*

You'll feed on the wealth of the nations. You want wealth? Step into Jesus' freedom. This is what God sent Jesus to do.

CHALLENGE

Here's what we've got to do. How do we get there? How do you get there? We have to take possession of it. We have to believe it!

The only way to make it deeper is to step out of the comfort zone and test it – is your foundational identity based on what God says or what others say?

Take It!

When God freed his people in Egypt, Moses sent out twelve spies. In Numbers 13, he sends out twelve spies. Ten of them come back and said, *"The people over there are powerful. Their cities were fortified and very large. We can't attack people because they are stronger than us."* You know what happened? Two of them were positive, crying that they could handle the pressure. The other ten weren't. The masses outweighed the two but the two were right. God sent them into the wilderness for forty years. They did not have to be there. It was never God's original plan for them to be in the wilderness for forty years.

Psalm 78:41 reviews all the Israelites' faults. It explains how they did not remember his power. Again, they place the Lord to the test. They vexed the Holy One of Israel, which means they limited God. Now some of you are whispering to yourselves, *"You can't limit God. That's not possible. What she's saying?"* That's in the word. They limited the Holy One of Israel. Why? Because they didn't remember his power and they didn't take it on the day he redeemed them from their oppressor. Matthew Henry's commentary explains that they limited God to their ways and their timing. They limited God to their ways and their timing.

We don't want to be those ten spies that didn't remember the power of God when they delivered us from the hand of the enemy and into the kingdom of God. We don't ever want to forget. He divided the sea for them and they didn't remember. I mean, you'd think, duh. Like how could you possibly not remember? Walking across on dry land after it was soaking wet—they didn't remember that. So when they went up against this giant or this obstacle or you know, my child's behind, all they saw was my child's behind. But they forgot to see, *"You know what, God brought me here. If he brought me here, he's going to take me through it. What sea do you need to divide today, God?"* John 16:33 stresses, *"In this world, you will have trouble. But take heart for I have overcome the world."*

Seriously, what? But take heart, it doesn't matter what mountain is before us. We have a choice. We have a choice. And we've got to be women that take possession of everything that Jesus Christ died for. Stand up. Wake up! Take it! We need to be women that take possession of what God has given us. No, we don't want to sit on our hands any longer and only moan and complain and be pitied. We shouldn't be complainers. I shouldn't complain about my body, because you know what, I don't do anything about it. I don't take possession of it. So shut your mouth if you're not going to take possession of it and let God be God.

Joshua was one of the two. He went in with two spies—they only sent two this time, I thought that was really smart. God said, *"I will give you every place that your foot sets."* That's you. Take it! That's your promise. Every place. Not the property, you're not going to get Walmart. But in your home you have the atmosphere control and you know that. You can take it down or you can bring it up. *"I'll bring you every place where your foot steps. No one will be able to stand against you all the days of your life."* All he said was, "Take possession of what I'm already giving you. Here's a gift. Take it. All you have to do is receive it."

But sometimes we don't know what we've received already and the price that Jesus paid. One drop of his blood was enough to free you, to make you an intimate friend. You don't need anybody else. You're not going to be rejected. He loves you so much. He's in love with you. He's proud of you. He knows you failed. He knows you yelled at your kids. He knows what you did. But you know what, he sees? Chosen, holy, blameless, loved. He loves you. You need to know that to your core because you cannot love your children until you know the love of God. You can sit down, but don't fall asleep. We need to wake up. And I'm not talking about physically wake up. We've got to stop being lukewarm. God puts a fire in our bones and we need to let it spray out. We should be persecuted a little bit more. We need to take possession of it. You know your identity in Him, you are healed, you treasure his word, you've revealed his power, now take it!

So God tells Joshua, *"Three days, you will go and take possession of the land your lord God is giving you for your own."* We have to take it. It's already given. He already gave us freedom. If you're in bondage, let it go in Jesus' name. Declare, *"God, thank you for freedom. Start thanking him.*

Thank you for binding my broken heart. Thank you for loving me." Start taking Isaiah 61 and voicing, *"Thank you, Jesus. Thank you, Jesus. Thank you, Jesus. You are enough."* I love that song. When you can't say anything else, simply say "Jesus." You can't go wrong. The effort does not need to be spoken. It took me a long time to learn that one. Jesus has everything, every power—he can transform anything in a moment. Your kids—bring them up to Jesus. Jesus. I'm going to say Jesus until you stop.

So Joshua told his men, *"All of you fighting men fully armed—,"* So he's telling them, we're going to take possession, but it's going to require some blood. This is going to be a fight. When you go to take possession of your emotions and your mind, when you go take possession of your body, it's going to be a war. It's not going to be easy. But it's going to be worth it. Hard things produce character in us, change us and transform us. It make us more into the image of God when we will stop submitting to our flesh and our insecurities and our fears.

So I am in my eighth year of homeschooling now. I'm at co-op that helps me a lot. Are you in a co-op? When you're in a co-op, all of a sudden, what happens, you start to see comparisons, right? You start to look at other kids and you're like, *"Wait a second, you're on algebra? We're still in multiplication."* "Your kid can read?" Or, *"Your kid can't read? But mine can."* You start to get this little bit of arrogance. You're exclaiming, *"Oh my gosh, this is so amazing."* I think that every day is an opportunity to look at what's in front of us and either be disappointed or prideful.

> *You don't have to beg God for freedom. He already gave it to you. You just need to step into it. Choose the abundant life. Step into freedom.*

For me, there were expectations I had that my kids would be really smart, that they would go to college, and that I would be able to teach them to read. I don't know how I'm going to but I'll be able to. When we're trying to do algebra and I realize, *"I can't remember how to do algebra.*

I need help," you start to feel like you are a failure, they're a failure. What am I going to do?

I had a dream to have a ten marriage. I once used this with my husband, *"I don't want a two marriage, I want a ten marriage."* You start off with a ten marriage, but then do you really end up with a ten marriage? One day, you're thinking like, *"I lied to you yesterday. But today, you didn't take out the trash. I don't like anything about you, and today our marriage is a two. You haven't pursued me; we haven't gone to a date. I'm tired, the house is a wreck. You don't see what I need."* It's so easy to look at our circumstances. It's so easy to say, *"Look at my child,"* and compare them to everyone else, *"They're not enough. They're not perfect. They're behind. They're not where they should be. My marriage isn't where it should be. I have too much debt. I have too much of everything."* Do you do that?

Out of our heart, our mouth speaks.

You might not have a child you're really proud of. You think you did a decent job but they're behind in math. They don't know they're behind in math until you don't tell them, right? I have a friend who posted on our homeschool loop that her kid is behind in math by two months and she's thinking of putting them back in public school. I exclaimed, *"Who told you that? Who told you your kid was behind in math? Who told you that? Who was it?"* When Adam sinned in the garden, he hid from God. Adam uttered, *"Hey. God I hid from you because I'm naked."* God said, *"Who told you that?"*

We have to know that there is an enemy who wants to come in and steal, kill and destroy us. He wants to take and destroy our image we have of our kids. He wants to destroy our kids' image through us. He wants to take it, to take them, from us! He wants us to compare and cry, *"My marriage sucks in comparison to yours. Your husband is actually better than mine. Look, your husband takes out the trash, he prays with you."*

But the enemy—I want you to hear this—he wants to take, kill, steal, and destroy you and your family. If you read John 10:10, you will remember that Jesus Christ came so you could have life and you can have life abundantly. That's what he came for. *"Oh, great, Sheri. Jesus came so I could have life and life abundantly. But what is that? What does that mean? What does it mean to have life and life abundantly? How does that* work in my everyday life? Because my life doesn't feel very abundant right now. My kids are behind in math, I do suck at teaching reading." It's really hard, because you're actually dealing with a human and you have to teach them. But the truth is, is that the truth wants to get into our thoughts and he wants to take over our thought life so that what we're thinking on will eventually come out of our mouth. But the enemy can't take it because you already have! Proverbs 18:21 says that the words have the power of life and death. Power of life and death. So as we're thinking on what we're lacking and what we're missing, we're not thinking on Jesus Christ. He came to bring us life and life abundantly. Take that life!

In Isaiah 61, it says *"God anointed me, Jesus, to preach the good news to the poor, to bind up the broken hearted, to proclaim freedom to the captives."* Are you in bondage to your own thoughts? Are you in bondage to the expectations that had been set before you? *"My kids have to have algebra too done by the end of the ninth grade?"* Are you in captive to those standards, *"My kid has to be reading by the time they are five or six?"* Are you in bondage to those standards that we have set before ourselves? Sometimes we have set them for each other. Jesus came to set us free from any standard but his.

He came to release us from darkness. Sometimes we're in prison to our own thought life. We're in a prison where we're constantly thinking on the negative. We're looking at our circumstance, we see a mountain and we think, *"Oh God, how am I going to make it over this hump? How am I going to lead my children over this mountain,"* right? We sing songs like, *"I will climb this mountain with arms open. God, I'll climb it. I'll do what you tell me to do. I will. I see it before me."*

But did you know, in Isaiah 45, Isaiah 41:15 and Zachariah 4:7 it says that God never intended you to climb a mountain. He said, *"I will give you a sharp new instrument with new teeth that will crush the mountain and it will become like chafe."* Take the instrument! Take it! I told someone once, *"You know what, you're in a valley. You're like this. You're so in the valley right now that you can't get out."* When we're in the valley, we can't get out on our own.

This morning, when I woke up, the Lord revealed to me, *"Hey remember, I made your path straight. I make the mountains molehills."* So

He starts to show me, *"I tell you, I will make the mountains go away."* So what does that leave you with? Oklahoma. Flat ground. A plain. It leaves me with a plain which took me to Psalm 91:1 to amplify this. *"He who rest in the shelter of the most high God will remain stable and fixed under the shadow almighty."* Jesus came to make our mountains a plain. We can speak to our mountains and command them to leave. But what we're doing as the body of Christ, and especially as a homeschool mother? We look and we see this mountain and, *"Okay, Lord, I'll climb the mountain. I will praise you over the mountain."* You know, *"I will, I'll praise you all through it. I'll climb the mountain."*

The enemy wants you to think you have to climb the mountain. But God sent Jesus Christ so he can destroy the mountain so that we can speak to the mountain. As long as we have the attitude that *"I have to climb the mountain, I have to look at my circumstances,"* and be daunted, then we are not going to take hold of life and life abundantly that Jesus Christ died to give us. Does that make sense?

You're this little tiny rudder of this that can turn your ship in a totally new direction. You don't ever have to go home and look at a mountain again and be discouraged. You don't need to climb mountain of discouragement—you know those days where you go, *"I want to move to China. Listen, honey, I packed my bags, I'm scheduling my flight, I'm moving to China and I'm leaving you here."* Have you ever felt like that? *"I don't want to do the laundry one more time. I don't want to teach you algebra."* It's too awful, right?

Well, Jesus Christ, in Isaiah 61, says that He came to bind up the broken-hearted. It's not something he does, it's what he did. His love, when he deposited his spirit into us, is readily accessible. We only have to take that spirit. Take it!

CHALLENGE

If you have a broken heart in a moment, he is there and he is present and he is ready to bind up the broken heart, your broken expectations, and your broken dreams. He is there to make it from a two to a ten. That's his promise. He came to comfort all who mourn. Proclaim it's the year of the Lord's labor. Bestow the crown of beauty instead of ashes; the oil of gladness instead of mourning.

Will you receive His healing right now?

"We demolish arguments and every pretension that sets itself up against the knowledge of God, and we take captive every thought to make it obedient to Christ."

2 Corinthians 10:5

Adopt It!

As you know, my parents were divorced when I was 3 years old. My mom remarried shortly after. When I was 5 years old, I was asked if I would like to be adopted by my stepdad. You see, my real dad was no longer in my life and the only dad I was ever going to know was my step-dad. I had no idea what being adopted meant so I asked. All I remember is that it meant changing my name. I told them I would think about it. I spent a few days in my room dreaming about my new name. On the 3rd day, I told my parents that I had made the decision to change my name. My step-dad was filled with excitement – he would soon be the dad of this *"Cutie patootie"*!

Then I burst out, *"I want to change my name to Deborahtha Ray!"* Oh, I imagined what a beautiful name I chose. I cannot wait for everyone to start calling me Deborahtha! I was so proud of my chosen new name! I don't remember the details from there, but no one called me Deborahtha – ever. I guess my beautiful name was rejected. I did not adopt it and neither did anyone else. Mom said that my stepdad was terribly disappointed.

Many of us know about adoption, but we don't really understand the fullness of adoption unless we have been or have adopted. Adoption is changing your name, yes. But it is also changing your family, your rights, your location, your privileges, your blood line; your parents. Adoption changes your Identity!

God brings everyone to the place where He asks you if you want to be adopted into His family! Many of us take days, weeks, and years to decide if we want to! Some never get it and think it's only about a name change.

We moved to Oklahoma when I was 9 years old. My mom signed me up for school with a new name, Sheri Hull. I insisted, *"Mom, that is not my name!"* Mom assured me, *"I know, but if you don't have the same name as I do than the school will not be able to easily contact me if something bad happens to you."* "If" and "bad" rang in my ears. Oh my! I didn't want people to not be able to find my mom! We were in a new state—away from all my family!

I adopted this new name until I was 15 years old.

Have you ever heard a rumor about yourself or had a reputation that, when you heard it, you knew that it was emphatically not true? As you know, my parents were divorced when I was three years old and I didn't see my dad's family for seven years after that. It was such a horrible breakup that no one got together anymore. So my mom told me a little bit about my grandma. She said when she lived with her, when I was a little girl, that my grandma would only make her a half a sandwich. She said she was really stingy with her food. When you live there with her, when you go see her, you'll starve, because you're so hungry, and there's nothing in the pantry, and she's really stingy with her food. She also told me that my grandmother was very strict.

So when I was ten years old, and I had to go visit my grandparents for the first time, I was scared. I thought, *"Okay, I'm going to go over there. I'm going to be starving. I'm not going to get anything to eat, and they're going to be really strict, and I won't know what I can touch or what I can do."* I'm merely this ten-year-old little kid. So the first time my mom dropped me off, I said, *"You come back in 60 minutes, not 61, 60 on the dot. I'm going to be watching the time."* So I stayed, and I visited with my grandparents.

The first impression that I had of them when I walked in was, *"You're so old."* I couldn't believe all the wrinkles on their bodies. I had never seen, actually, an old person that looked that old before in real life. So I was scared of my grandparents. I was scared because I thought they were strict. I was scared because I thought that they were stingy, and then they were old, and I really, honestly thought they were going to die while I was visiting. I thought, *"Mom, get back before they die."* They're going to be so old.

I had a view of my grandmother through my mother's eyes, and some of us have a twisted view of God like I had of my grandmother. We wear these spiritual goggles like the old person goggles that I was wearing. To truly be able to see my grandmother, I had to actually get to know her. I had to spend time with her to learn who she was. That's the same thing we have to do with God. I had to spend time to learn that my view of God that was given to me by another person wasn't actually true. We have to put on our spiritual goggles so that we can go diving and check out and see who God really is. Maybe our view of God has been twisted because of what someone else believes. We've seen God through their vision, through their experience, and not through our own, and God didn't design us for that.

I want to share with you a verse from Psalm 86:5, and it says, *"You are forgiving and good, oh, Lord, abounding in love to all who call on You."* That is a good God. When we look through our spiritual goggles at that verse, we see the sweetness of God. Our view of God—it can be changed. If we look at God, and we think, *"Oh, God, He's not merciful. He's unforgiving. He's unloving. He's stingy. He's too strict."* Maybe our view of God is like my view of my grandma.

There's another verse from James 1:17 which says, *"Every good and perfect gift is from above."* From above, every good gift that you've ever received is from God Himself. He's the author of it. How cool is that? Maybe you thought the bad gifts that you received were from God, but this Scripture tells us, *"Every good and perfect gift is from God."* God's original design for us was that our birth certificates would actually have His name on it.

In Ephesians 1:5, it says that, *"He predestined us to be adopted as sons and daughters through Jesus Christ in accordance with His good will."* John 1:12-13 also says that, *"We are now children of God. Not born of natural descent nor human decision or a husband's will. No longer a product of the flesh, of our parents, but we are born of God."* I've got a news flash

> *When you got saved, you were adopted by God and He gave you a new birthright. His name is now on your birth certificate as Father and gave you the key to His Kingdom.*

today. You have been adopted into God's family, and this Bible is your adoption manual. This has everything you need to know about what it's like to be a child of God.

A long time ago, 20-something years, we got our first VCR. Before we had VCRs, we had never plugged anything into the TV before. I remember my parents getting the VCR out of the box, and they sat and looked at their instructions for hours to try to figure out how to plug this thing in, and then how does it work, and how do you actually record or play movies. They spent an entire day figuring out what we can all do in less than 30 minutes today. The only reason why they were able to accomplish setting up the VCR is because they had a manual. It was very thorough. Today, they do a much better job with instruction, but this is very crucial to our walk with Christ. This is everything we need to know about being a child of God.

The first thing I want to look at is your new family. Once you're born again through Jesus Christ, you get a new birth certificate. The Bible actually says, *"You are a new creation."* John 5:24 actually says, *"You have crossed over out of death."* Your old life—that life before you believed on Christ—it is actually dead. You were living in death, and so when you're born again, you cross over out of death into life. That is awesome news.

> "THE SPIRIT YOU RECEIVED DOES NOT MAKE YOU SLAVES, SO THAT YOU LIVE IN FEAR AGAIN; RATHER, THE SPIRIT YOU RECEIVED BROUGHT ABOUT YOUR ADOPTION TO SONSHIP. AND BY HIM WE CRY, "*ABBA, FATHER.*"[16] THE SPIRIT HIMSELF TESTIFIES WITH OUR SPIRIT THAT WE ARE GOD'S CHILDREN."
>
> **Romans 8:15-16**

So you've crossed out over slavery, *"that was bondage to fear,"* and now you've crossed into life, *"and you received a Spirit of adoption. The Spirit producing sonship, daughtership, the sonship, your child, in we cry, 'Abba, Father.'"* When you look at your birth certificate where it says mother and father, now it says, *"Abba, Father."* That is in your adoption manual.

I love how Jesus talks about it in Mark 4. He's teaching a large group of people, and the crowd says, *"Hey, your mother and your brothers and your sisters, they're outside waiting for you."* In their mind, they're thinking, *"These people are really important. They're Your bloodline relationship. You need to stop what You're doing, because Your bloodline is far more important than what You're doing right here. You need to go see them."* Well, Jesus replied, and He said to them, *"You see, here are my mothers, my brothers and sisters. Whoever does the things God willed is my mother, my brother, and my sister."* Jesus knew that he was the Son of God. He was naturally born of Mary, and He had natural brothers and sisters, but He knew His birth certificate was Abba, Father, and so is ours. So is mine, and so is yours. We've got to start putting on our spiritual goggles so that we can see what family we belong to. We have to adopt it!

So we've looked at our birth certificate, and now we're going to look at our birthright. When you're born of God, there's a birthright given to you. After I was about ten years old, I started spending time with my grandmother. For ten years, honestly, almost nine to ten years, I was very hesitant in my relationship with her. I never spent more than 60 to 90 minutes at their house. Not a minute late, because I did not know them, and I didn't take the time to get to know them. I looked at them through the view of my mother for so long.

But one week in college, I decided, *"You know what? I'm going to take a week of my life off of work, off of school, and I'm going to go spend it with my grandparents to get to know who they are."* I had

You are called, justified, glorified, and chosen.

never spent the night at their house before, and I stayed an entire week. My grandparents had a four-story home. It was awesome. It was beautiful, and had tons of rooms and Ping-Pong table and books and games and movies and treasures I never knew that they actually had there. I also found out that they had a membership to a country club. I had never been to a country club before. We were very poor, and I didn't know it, but my grandparents were rich. I had no idea, because I hadn't spent any time with them to know it.

Every morning, my grandpa took me out to breakfast. Every day, he taught me all the things he knew about finances, which was unbelievable, and my grandmother wasn't stingy with the food. I got into the refrigerator anytime I wanted. It was such a relief to me, and they weren't strict. They were actually amazing! I learned that I could go swimming at the country club, drive the golf cart, and eat any snack I wanted to. It was so freeing to know that I had all of that all along. It was as if it was my birthright, what I was supposed to have. I was supposed to be in that family from the first day of my life. I would've always known what it was like to be their grandchild had it played out that way. It was like my birthright had been restored to me. I had been adopted.

Well, that is exactly what God does through our adoption manual. He restores our birthright. What was originally intended for us, before Adam and Eve sinned, He gives it all back through Jesus Christ. He restores it all when we believe in Him. He actually gives us the keys to His Kingdom. They're in here. I can't go through them all, but the keys to the Kingdom are in here. You need to know this. This adoption manual, it is life to you. You have to open it and know for yourself so that you can know who your Father is and your birthright.

I'm going to go through a few of the ones I love from Romans 8. First of all, with your birthright is there's no condemnation. You're set free. You have the Spirit of Christ. Christ is in you. You're a son or a daughter of God. You're an heir of God, an heiress. When my grandparents passed away, I inherited treasures that they had. An inheritance is something that comes at the death of the giver, not at the death of the receiver. Our inheritance from Christ is now. We've already received it; we only have to adopt it!

Romans 8 also says that we are called, justified, glorified, chosen, and He graciously gives us all things.

> "GREATER LOVE HAS NO ONE THAN THIS, THAT HE THAT LAYS DOWN HIS LIFE FOR HIS FRIENDS."
>
> **John 15:13**

No one in your life, no one that you're busy with, having tea with or coffee with will lay their life down for you, but Jesus Christ did. Your birthright is that you are loved. No one can ever reject you out of His love.

Another verse is a news flash to me. We're rich. A lot of us have financial difficulties. We've maybe overspent. We've spent too much, and we haven't been effective stewards of our finances, but I want you to know that your Abba, Father is rich. This is kind of an awkward-worded verse, but I love it. It is Psalm 50:10, and it says, *"For every beast of the forest is Mine."* This is God talking. Every beast of the forest is His. *"And the cattle upon a thousand hills and upon the mountains where they are."* They're all God's. Everything you see is God's. We might selfishly hold onto it, but it's all God's. He is able to provide for every financial need. He's able to restore when you've broken His commands.

Another birthright is that you're empowered. Ephesians 1:17-21 are some of my favorite verses. God gives us His Holy Spirit. In Ephesians, it says, *"May we know the Spirit, the power that lives in and for us, the same power that raised Christ from the dead."* We have that empowerment.

Another one of my favorite birthrights is that we're protected. This is an awesome revelation, and I don't want you to miss this.

> "BEHOLD! I HAVE GIVEN YOU AUTHORITY AND POWER TO TRAMPLE UPON SERPENTS AND SCORPIONS."
>
> **Luke 10:19**

Let me restate this verse in another way that you might understand it a little bit better. *"I have given you authority and power to trample upon serpents and scorpions, the physical, mental strength and ability over all the power that the enemy possesses, and nothing will harm you in any way. Nothing will harm you in any way."* That's what this adoption manual says. I'm in the Kingdom of God. I am a child of God. I'm no longer connected to my old bloodline. I'm connected to the power of God through the Holy Spirit that lives in me through His Son Jesus Christ, and nothing shall harm me in any way.

"And so I will inherit a double portion in my land, and everlasting joy will be mine. You are for me not against me."

CHALLENGE

Copy your Birth Certificate. Write in the mother and father lines, "God." Now do that for others in your household. Share this around the table, with your small group, friends, or family. Those with parent pains will feel renewed knowing that John 1:12-13 is their inheritance.

"Yet to all who did receive him, to those who believed in his name, he gave the right to become children of God--children born not of natural descent, nor of human decision or a husband's will, but born of God."

Jonn 1:12-13 NIV

See It!

You might be in the wilderness right now because God shown you his promise and you've said something like, *"It's too big, it's too hard, I can't do it."* Maybe you can't see it. But I feel like I'm one of the two spies. I've spied the promises of God. I've spied the Promised Land with my own eyes and my own life. And I looked in and said, *"Oh my gosh, it's so nice over here. Come and join me. Don't look at it and think it's too hard because your God will fight for you. He is your way; it is a well you didn't dig."* I'm one of the two spies. I don't know what spy you are, but we have to jump in with the two spies and be somebody who can take possession of the promises that God has already given to us through Jesus which is life and life abundantly.

The thief comes to steal, kill and destroy. Are you a helper of the thief in your own home on days where you're stealing for your kids' confidence? You're stealing from them and you're actually cooperating with the thief. John 16 says, *"In this world you'll have trouble. But take heart for I have overcome the world."* That's taking possession. It's *"Hey, trouble's going to come at me. This isn't going to be an easy journey, but I'm going to stand, feet firmly planted in the promises of God."*

> *Renew your mind with the Word. The more you read the word, the more you can see it: Your* **INDJC** *– identity in Jesus Christ! It will cause your heart and thoughts to change, and eventually, your words will change. All of this equals a powerfully changed life.*

Did you know God parted the red sea for the Israelites? And when they were in the wilderness, they forgot. Do you remember that? Okay, I can understand forgetting. Like, God helped me flush my toilet one time. My toilet wouldn't flush. *"I don't want to plunge the toilet."* I thought, *"Well, wait. God loves me. God, could you plunge the toilet? Would you help this thing flush? I know you love me so much. My husband would do it for me, you're better than him."* When I laid my hands on it and I said, *"Toilet, flush in Jesus name,"* and it flushed. I remember that. I can't imagine, what if the Red Sea parted, would I ever forget that? I saw it.

But in Psalm 78:41, which you need to know because you gotta look at your own life, it says, *"Again and again that they put God to the test and they vexed the Holy One of Israel."* It means they limited God. The Israelites actually limited God. He divided the sea and made it stand. He guided them by cloud. He brought them water out of a rock, okay? He did all of these things, but they continued to sin against Him. It actually says that they forgot what God had done in their lives and it made God angry. God's in control. But you can limit God in your life. The Matthew Henry commentary says that they limited God to their way and their timing. Have you done that before? God can't do this. You guys are probably thinking, *"God didn't flush your toilet."* I would never do that, because, I asked. I didn't have any limits on God at that moment. If you take the limits off of God, what sea does he need to part for you? He's willing to part it and he's powerful enough to part it. That's who he is. He's the God who parts the seas for us and makes it on dry ground. It's miraculous if we actually see it.

They saw it. God showed them, *"Here's the Promised Land. This is the great land I have for you. All you have to do is go in and take possession of it."* That is what God is telling us. *"This is the great and abundant life I have for you that you don't have to look at your circumstances and be daunted by them."*

They may be tough, but every day, I can say, *"You know what, in this world, I may have trouble, but take heart, Jesus, you overcame the world. Jesus I trust you."* When you do that, you start to get joy and you start to get hope. You start to be a functional mother. When you look at your child that's behind in math, you can voice, *"You're beautiful and you're smart. And you know what, God has a calling for you that he has already equipped you for and I'll help him pull it out."* Then your children become what you speak into them. So if you're speaking that *"You're behind, you're behind, you're behind,"* they're going to stay behind. But if you start to take possession of the promises of God or the Promised Land, your heart will change, your thoughts will change, and your words will change. Your life will change. Your children will change. Your marriage will change. Your neighbors will change. Your friends will change. You hear me? Does any of that need to change in your life? Do you need to see it?

We're verbalizing things like what Israelites did. *"I want to go back into slavery. My belly was full. It was an easy life over there."* You get over into your own strength and we lose it and we tear down because we look and we see with our natural eyes. We see mountains; we see daunting tasks before us. But God is saying, *"You're my chosen people."* The Israelites were His chosen people and His own people didn't believe his word. Even though his promise had been out there for hundreds of years, they didn't believe it.

> *When you know your identity in Jesus Christ, it changes you.*

Well, you are God's chosen people. He is saying, *"I don't want your kids to be like you. I want them to be better than you. I want your ceiling to be their floor."* How high is your ceiling? How you do that is you, in your life, take possession of those promises of God.

I call my husband a flat liner. He doesn't move. He doesn't blip on the radar, nothing upsets him either way. I want to date my husband. I want to have that ten marriage I told you about before. I want to have a fiery awesome marriage. One day I asked him, I said, *"I don't want a two, do you want a two?"* And he replied, *"I thought we had a ten."* I said, *"Huh, ha ha ha. Wow. You think we have a ten, I think we have a two."* It only took me stepping in and saying "I'm going to have a ten marriage. I will have a ten marriage. My name is Sheri Yates and I'm going to have a ten marriage. You know how I had a ten marriage?" I loved my husband. I speak truth into him, I take the word of God and I regurgitate it back to him. I assert, *"You are a man who climbs city walls and tear down strongholds which men trust. And everything is obliterated except for God himself as who they trust in."* I simply start speaking that stuff over him. I'll tell him, *"You know what, I know the clients aren't rolling in fist over fist, but guess what, they're coming because God's promises are true. This is what he said and this will come to pass."* My marriage starts exploding when my mind makes a shift to take possession of God's word and his truth.

You know, I think a lot of times, we are begging God. You know, *"God be with me. God help me. God be my source, be my friend, be closer to me. I want more of you God."* Have you ever said that? *"God I want more of you."* But did you know you're never going to get any more of God? When you are born again, He gave you all of Him. He deposited His Holy Spirit in you. He didn't give you a fourth and me a tablespoon and you a full dose. His word says He gave us His Holy Spirit and deposited it into us and sealed us. Sealed shut. If it can't come out, can you really get more? Can you see it?

> *Begin taking possession of God's promises because they belong to you.*

The scripture reveals that we have everything we need for life and godliness through the knowledge of God. So we've got all of them, but we get there by renewing our minds with the word. The more we get the word, the more knowledge that we get, the more we tap into the power.

Paul in Ephesians 1:17, he didn't pray you more of God, he prayed that you have more revelation of God; that you would have the spirit of wisdom and revelation to know God more deeply and intimately. He never prayed for somebody to have more. It's more understanding of what they've already had. The more you understand what you already have, it's going to change you because we're praying the wrong prayers to take possession. *"God, send your presence with me."* If He's not entering you, then He's already here. He's saying, *"Acknowledge my presence. There's power in my presence and I'm with you all the time. I never left you, I never forsook you."* Phew. Breathe.

When you know your identity in Jesus Christ, it changes you. It changes everything. Because when you know you're free, you're free to choose, you're free to choose to not sin, you're free to choose love or you're free to choose hate, you get the choice; the freedom sets you free to choose rightly if you see it and believe it.

God isn't commanding you to love him or to choose him. He's let his hands go there wide open. They're flat. *"You choose. If you choose me, it's awesome. But I want you. Will you say yes?"* It's that simple. The ability to choose—it changes everything. It sets you free completely. There's no slavery in the liberty of choice.

> *Freedom sets you free to choose rightly.*

Boundaries are a tool when one cannot handle independence responsibly. Some people need boundaries. But the truth is, boundaries act like a law and the law activates your flesh and your flesh activates sin. God has given you boundary-less opportunity to love and to choose him, to walk free of shackles. If you can't handle the choice without hurting others, then you certainly require boundaries. You need a jail cell like a convict – a place that protect others from your reckless behavior. In Christ, you are completely free from the law.

Let's look at grace and mercy. Mercy is not getting the punishment that I deserve. Grace is getting a free gift I didn't earn. I don't deserve it. It's a free gift.

One of my friends had a daughter that had a crisis and I got to walk with her through that crisis. I mentored her, loved her, and literally walked with her. We talked scripture together. She told me what she was going through. When she came on to the other side with her total freedom, her dad wanted to bless me in some way and thank me for the time I spent with his daughter. He bought me an Apple laptop. Wow. It was a pretty big gift to receive. I never really received that big of a gift ever in my life except my wedding ring.

> *In Christ, you are completely free from the law.*

It's really hard for us to receive free gifts when we haven't earned them or worked for them because we're such a working society. We think, *"I put in my eight hours. Pay me for my time, I've earned it. Pay me what I'm due."* But if we were paid for what we were due from God, we all are due a sentence of death. We're due a sentence of life in prison and confinement, because not one of us is good without him. Not a single hair in our head, a cell in our body is good apart from the Lord.

God himself, although we deserve death, He gave us mercy, which through his son Jesus Christ, he sent him so that we could be free from that sentence of death and confinement and slavery. That is mercy. Mercy is not getting the punishment that we deserve. We deserve death, and God sent his son so that we could have life. That life is grace. Not getting death is mercy, but not only do we not get death, but he sent his son in John 10:10 to give us life and life abundantly which is a gift of grace. It's receiving a gift we didn't earn or deserve. It's over the top. It's not just payment, but it's a gift in addition to.

When we understand that gift fully and we know we've been completely restored and completely forgiven, that there's not anything in our past that God's remembering and holding against us, he's not mad at us, Isaiah 54:9 says he's not disappointment in you as much as you think he might be, as much as your friends have told you God is, he's not. He's looking at you as his righteous child of God. He is the righteousness of Christ. A new creation.

Yes, we can improve on things, on the things that we do, but we are human beings, not human doings. God called us to be and exist in him and to know him. The more that we know him and the more that we seek him, the more he's going to make us complete in all our gifts.

If we have a lack in our doing and we have a gap in our ability, then we need to go back to the one who gives the ability, the one who gives the gifts. The call of God is irrevocable. We're supposed to be seeking all the gifts all the time. If you understand that someone is not walking in the fullness of their identity, you should be calling them to war and pray and step into their true identity and seek God for all the gifts.

Where you're lacking, God can make you able. We can't preach from the pulpit that God equips the called and then say you don't have the equipment to do this. There's a problem there. If we don't have the equipment, then we need to go back to the Lord and find out what we need to do differently.

Truly, when you understand that, you don't need boundaries. The love of God explodes in your heart and you begin to follow him and obey him out of that love. John 14:15 says, *"If you love me, you'll obey my commands."* I don't obey God to prove that I love him. No, it's out of the love you have for him, and because of what he's done for you that create a response that equal obedience to him. That response brings you freedom. You don't want to sin anymore. You don't want to be in bondage to slavery or pornography or hate or unforgiveness. I don't want to be in bondage to bitterness. I've already done that. I've lived that life and it's painful. It hurts. Every day in your life, you're holding a grudge on someone. It eats at you from the inside out. It's like cancer in your soul.

Understanding God's expansive love for you will reveal to you that you are loved. My identity is not: slave, unworthy, unloved, rejected, and abandoned. It's I am loved. I am loved completely and holy so ridiculously. I've received the greatest gift and the greatest forgiveness. Because of that, I don't need boundaries. I need my God and he directs my steps. He changes my path. He's constantly making my crooked ways straight. Every step I take, I rest in that and I have the fullness of joy and peace every step of my life, whether I'm doing right or messing up. That is freedom.

CHALLENGE

Can you see God's love for you? Do you know it in your head only or in your heart? If you are not yet overwhelmed with how He feels about you, spend some quiet time with Him and rest in His love for you until you see it clearly.

Stop It!

Anyone who's ever been to my house knows I am a stay at home mom that homeschools, but I'm not really adept at things that matter for a home maker. I'm a CPA and I had planned to be a partner in my firm. That was my plan. I would be a partner and my kids would attend daycare. But the first day I laid my child down in the crib at daycare, I lost it. I was an emotional basket case! It didn't feel right! My thoughts stumbled – *This is unnatural. I don't think this is how God designed me."* I went to work and sobbed – all day…every day. At the time, I was a manager in a public accounting firm in downtown Oklahoma City and I sat there and, *"Whaa!"*

The begging began at home, "Honey, would you please let me quit my job." Hubs firmly had his own opinion, "No, you're going to be a partner. Stick with it. Eventually, you will want this too." I whined, complained, cried, pouted, because I was building my case because I was determined to quit my career. I left work daily at 2:30 to pick up my first born because I couldn't tolerate any more hours away from her precious life!

If you look at my house, you'll see that I may not be cut out of the cloth to be that Suzie Homemaker—you know, the hospitality gift or the clean woman. It's really easy for me to put myself down and measure against those other women who do a fantastic job at keeping their home sparkly.

Well, given that I don't have a gift of housekeeping, the co-op that I'm a part of assigned us a job every year. In one of the jobs that they assigned me for an entire year was cleaning up the bathrooms. I had to clean up the girls' bathroom which is pretty decent. I mean, girls usually hit the target, right? They're pretty clean, you know, they wipe off their hands after everything, but I have to clean the boys' bathroom. If you have boys, you know that they don't really hit it all the time. They miss it and the bathroom is full of urinals. So going in there, you need to tie two socks around your nose. It's so stinky.

One day, a little girl made a project with all these beautiful horses on it. The boys got a little angry and took the horses. They ripped it off and decided they're going to flush them down the toilet. Well, one horse was stuck. He's crying out in the depths of the toilet, "Help me!" and I'm the bathroom lady. So I don't like to clean. And I'm in the stinky bathroom, socks tied around my head, and I ponder, "How am I going to get this horse out of the toilet?" I've got to do it. It's my job, it's my responsibility. So it dawns on me—trash bags. I've got a brilliant idea. Yes. This is what I'll do. Oh, I'm going in. It's like my arm literally wrapped up to here. I'm afraid, you know, to get it too deep. I plunged my hand down into the toilet and it's crammed in there. I'm thinking, please don't break. It's in the boys' toilet. I reached my hand down and I wiggled that horse loose, I bring it out and I was like, *"Yeah!"* I'm pretty proud of myself. I went down into the depths of the sewer to collect this horse.

Stop settling for your old identity.

Finally, you've got to study your identity. Our kids need to know that they are not defined by what other people say. They are not defined by what they do. They are not defined by what has happened to them. They are not defined by what you say. They're defined by God. Their identity is to find in Him and Him alone. We've got to know our identity in Christ and if you know me, that's my platform. Without knowing your identity in Christ, you're really in rough waters. As James says, *"You're in the water being tossed to and fro."* People are going to say, *"You did an impressive job today, Sheri,"* and then someone else is going to state, *"That really stunk, it was horrible."* I could go back and forth, saying, *"I'm sad." "I'm happy!"* I don't care because my God's called me and I am chosen and I am confident in that. That is an amazing freedom and I want every one of God's children on this entire earth to walk in that kind of confidence because it truly allows you to love the unlovable. It allows you to love the person who persecutes you. That's the kind of freedom that studying your identity in Christ will get you.

Stop letting the enemy deceive you.

You can't receive the truth until you recognize the lie, because the lie is more truth to you than the truth. It is imperative that we look into our own hearts and dig out those old hurts and those old wounds and keep putting. If you put in God's truth enough, eventually it will eventually drown out the lie. If you keep God's truth in, keep hammering it and going, *"I'm chosen. I'm holy. I'm blameless. I am innocent. I am clean. I am not ashamed. I am not that dirty, disgusting rag that I thought I was as a kid, I'm not stupid. I have the mind of Christ"*, those thorns will come out!

Sometimes we simply need to stop it and remember all that we've been through. We know our identity; we are healed and revealed, teachers and thrashers. It's time to stop it and just *be*. Scripture tells us in Colossians 3:15 to *"Let the peace of Christ rule in our hearts. Since we're members of one body,"* and my favorite part of that verse is, *"and be thankful."* The best way to stop thinking about the lies and the thief and the discouragements in our life is to be thankful.

I was sitting across from a baby the other day and she was crying, *"Wah!"* She was throwing a whopping fit. You can see the mom was thinking, *"What, what does she need? What does she need?"* The sisters were the same, "What does she need, what does she need?" All of a sudden, the baby's spots a toy, grabs it and became happy. Being thankful can distract us from the negative things that we are thinking on, like a baby is distracted when we give them a toy. Does that make sense?

Stop it! Stop stinkin' thinkin' and be thankful. Somebody challenged me to do a thankful list. I don't know if you've read it but it's called A Thousand Gifts. I never read it, but somebody challenged me to be thankful and write them down. So I started a thankful journal. This is my second one. I have about 1,400 things that I'm thankful for. When you change your thoughts to being thankful, it is amazing how it changes your life. My children have all started one and I have one that is over a thousand. So we can stop our stinkin' thinkin' by being thankful.

Here's the deal: We can stop the stinkin' thinkin', but it takes a while before you can replace it with the truth. I was thinking about this and I thought about a trash

Stop letting the enemy discourage you.

dump. At a trash dump, people and trash trucks keeps coming, dropping off the trash. Let's say we have a vision for that trash dump to be a park. We would need to stop bringing the trash there and then we would need to overhaul the area. So I started thinking about, *"That's what replacing trash with truth is like!"*

The first thing we need to do is to stop stinkin' thinkin'. Stop letting people place trash in us. Stop letting enemy deceive you. Stop letting the enemy discourage you. And then comes the hard work. Now we've got this whole area of trash we need to renovate. It needs to be renewed as Romans 12:2 conveys, *"We're transformed with the renewing of the mind."* Think about renovating the house, renovating that property. Imagine in your head is a giant trash dump and it is full of trash. We've got to bring in bulldozers. We've got to bring in equipment and we've got to start thinking it over because all the old trash is still present. That's what exactly happens to us. Our mind is filled up with all the lies we believed until today.

It's filled. Full. People have put them in you, the devil has put it in you, and you have probably voiced them to yourself in your mirror. It's full of garbage and the only way to renovate it is to set God's word in. But it takes so much time and it takes hard work, right? It takes hard work to get that stuff stirred up and added there until it is fine soil. It takes commitment. It takes a decision to speak, *"No more. I'm turning the trash dump in my mind into a place where God can put his word."*

When God showed up in my life and revealed to me that he loved me, I thought, *"I don't know that I've ever really been loved. How can you love me?"* I struggled with that for so long. You only have your earthly parents to compare God to, but they're nothing. Your earthly parents are nothing like God.

Start claiming the promises of God and be thankful.

> "THE ACCUSER OF OUR BROTHERS WHO ACCUSES THEM BEFORE GOD DAY AND NIGHT HAS BEEN HURLED DOWN."
>
> **Revelations 12:10**

"For the accuser," know who the accuser is? It's the devil, it's the enemy, and it's the thief who wants to steal from you. The enemy is constantly accusing us. The voice that's there when you sleep, when you wake, constantly accusing you. It's constantly lying to you. It's constantly bringing you those six Ds. Here's the good news. We know the end of the story. The end is he doesn't win. If you knew the outcome of the game you bet on it beforehand so you could get a huge cash inflow, right? If I knew the lottery numbers right now, I would go pick them, right? You know the end of the story. You know the only power he has over you is deceit, is to pull you down by your ankles. It's time to proclaim, *"No more. I'm going to stop my stinkin' thinkin'. I'm going to stop it."*

You can tell yourself that. You can preach to yourself, *"I'm going to stop it and I'm going to start to take the word of God and I am going to install it in. No more trash in me, in Jesus' name. I'm not receiving it."* It's going to take you time, so that's why you stop it first. Be thankful because it takes a long time to realize I'm really chosen.

My platform since the beginning, really honestly, of my ministry in Christ is about identity and who we are in Christ. That's what changed my life. What changed my life was knowing God and knowing that I was his daughter and that everything that happened to me that was bad in my past, it didn't have to have any claim on me anymore. I was free. That has been my platform. I mean, my license plate reads IDNJC. My reputation is identity in Jesus Christ.

When I sat down to write my first book, Stuck, I was thinking, *"This does not make any sense. Why would I start with this hook? What in the world is going on?"* I really wanted to have a book out by an event that I was doing. So it started and I went for it a hundred miles an hour, ducked my heels in; worked on it. Got Stuck finished and now it's out. I get phone calls from people now asking, *"Hey, can you help me write my book?"*

"Can you read my book?" "Give me some inspiration or some motivation." One of my favorite things to do is to help people achieve their dreams!

I love to see people succeed. I love to see people soar. I love to see people click and get it and go on their own. I love to see people thrive. I love, love, love, love when people accomplish something that their family never did; that they break barriers that shock the generations that went before them and it has been a blast. Now I'm thinking, *"God, you are so tricky. I wrote stuck because my heart's desire is to help people know you and make you known."* What better way to do that than write a book that helps people take the dreams God has placed in their heart and launch them into something incredible into the book they've always wanted to do into movie, into a screenplay, into a song they've always wanted to write, into serving the homeless that they've always wanted to, into going to college, into whatever. I'm so grateful that man has these plans but God directs his steps.

"Stop it. Stop it or I'm going to bury you alive in a box."

It's one of my favorite lines from a Bob Newhart movie that's still on YouTube today, if you want to google it.

But it's really true—when I think about how many people live the day settled living in their old identity. They settled in living a life that isn't life and life abundantly like God provided for them. They settled and it's time to stop it.

CHALLENGE

It's time to stop settling in your old identity. It's time to stop living out of the past. It's time to stop keeping a record of wrongs. It's time to stop not receiving what God has for you. It's time to stop blaming all your problems on God. It's time to stop faltering every time a mountain gets in your way. It's time to start speaking to mountains. It's time to start claiming the promises of God because his answer to them is always yes and amen. It's time to stop it. Write down your conviction to stop it!

Start IT!

It's time to start taking God's Word's to heart and eating it – quite literally! Let HIM only be true and every single other man – including yourself – be a BIG FAT LIAR!

The only way to do this is to change the direction of your thinking. Stinkin' Thinkin' must GO! Kick it out! Ditch the labels! Take possession of your new name by reading and believing your adoption manual – the BIBLE!

The Bible calls it "renewing" your mind. It means to reprogram. Make new. Clean the slate with new thoughts.

In one radical version, 2 Corinthians 10:5 says to **LEAD** your thoughts into obedience of Christ!

That's a thought – LEAD YOUR THOUGHTS. Our thoughts are too often a run-away train of our fears and flesh. Lies! Lies! Lies!

Today, turn! Turn around away from all that junk by starting something new!

To stop, you only have to START something new. I love this mind-renewing video created by Elevation Church (http://elevationchurch.org) Check it out: http://vimeo.com/54866496

Identity in Christ is the key to stability.

Even when you don't measure up to your true identity, it is still who you are! Start speaking to your future and watch what God will do through your renewed mind!

I love tools that help me remember what to do. I pray these tools help you!

- Exam it! – Examine your heart - your words – Do you know your IDNJC?
- Reprogram it! – Reprogram your mind.
- Start it! – Start taking your thoughts captive.
- Shut it! – Shut your mouth because you speak death over yourself (or anyone else for that matter)
- Ditch it! – Ditch the labels. Leave the past in the past. Forgive yourself if you messed up because God already forgave you. You don't believe it? See John 3:16-17.
- Read it! – Read the Bible to get Truth circulating in your thought life.
- Believe it! – Believe the Word of God. Let it be your reality more than your circumstance.
- Receive it – let God heal your broken heart
- Take it! – Take possession of your new identity with passion! Own it! Be it! Shine it!
- Remember it! – Remember that's not who you are. Words can be thrown at you, but you don't have to receive them anymore!
- Bind it – when someone speaks against you, send those words packing. Break agreement with them!
- Shake it! – Shake off he words people speak to you in line with your old ID.
- Don't break it! – Don't void the words you have been speaking and planting in your heart by trash talking yourself.

After you GET IT…..

- Share it - share with others. Give it away. Let people know how God sees them! This is your mission field.

Identity in Christ is the key to stability. To kick-start your new view of yourself, I am providing you with this key tool!

God's Word is life to our whole self!

> "MY SON, ATTEND TO MY WORDS; CONSENT AND SUBMIT TO MY SAYINGS. LET THEM NOT DEPART FROM YOUR SIGHT; KEEP THEM IN THE CENTER OF YOUR HEART. FOR THEY ARE LIFE TO THOSE WHO FIND THEM, HEALING AND HEALTH TO ALL THEIR FLESH."
>
> Proverbs 4:20-22 (Amp)

Read through the following confession and I am chart every day. Write them on your hands, mirror, sticky notes, place them in your child's lunch box, write them in notes to friends, read them aloud, write yourself notes with these truths. You don't have to remember the LIES you have believed about yourself. No. All you need to do is start hearing what God thinks of you and eventually it will take root in your heart. Trust me…you will be forever changed!

IDNJC Confession

Today, I choose to believe You, God above the opinions of others or my opinions of myself. I love myself through Your Truth, Father. I no longer see myself based on my circumstances, weaknesses, or inadequacies. I leave the past behind me so that I can look forward and see what You are doing right now!

I listen and hear Your voice. I will be fully present. Because I am a secure, loved child of God, I see clearly how deeply He loves others! I will obey Your voice the first time. Because I love You, Father, I obey You. All of these things are sealed in Jesus' name!

I Am Chart

I AM and that's all I need to know!
I am God's possession. (Gen. 17:8; 1 Cor. 6:20)
I am God's child. (John 1:12)
I am God's workmanship. (Eph. 2:10)
I am God's friend. (James 2:23)
I am God's temple. (1 Cor. 3:16, 6:16)
I am God's vessel. (2 Tim. 2:2)
I am God's laborer. (1 Tim. 5:18)
I am God's witness. (Acts 1:8)
I am God's soldier. (2 Tim. 2:3)
I am God's ambassador. (2 Cor. 5:20)
I am God's building. (1 Cor. 3:9)
I am God's chosen. (Eph. 1:4)
I am loved by God. (Rom. 1:7; 2 Thes. 2:13)
I am God's heritage. (1 Pet. 5:3)
I am complete in Christ. (Col. 2:10)
I am forever free from sin's power. (Rom. 6:14)
I am sanctified. (1 Cor. 6:11)
I am loved eternally. (1 Pet. 1:5)
I am kept in the palm of His hand. (John 10:29)
I am kept from falling. (Jude 1:24)
I am not condemned. (Rom. 8:1-2; 1 Cor. 11:32)

I am one with the Lord. (1 Cor. 6:17)
I am quickened by His mighty power. (Eph. 2:1)
I am seated in heavenly places. (Eph. 1:3)
I am light in the darkness. (Matt. 5:14)
I am a candle in a dark place. (Matt. 5:15)
I am beautiful. (Ps. 45:10-11)
I am His. (Is. 43:1)
I am a city set on a hill. (Matt. 5:14)
I am a citizen of Heaven. (Phil. 3:20; 1 Pet. 2:11)
I am hidden with Christ. (Ps. 32:7)
I can do all things through Christ. (Phil. 4:13)
I find mercy and grace in Him. (Heb. 4:16)
I can pray always and everywhere. (Luke 21:36)
Fiery darts of the wicked one are quenched with my shield of faith. (Eph. 6:16)
I boldly approach the Father. (Heb. 10:19)
I can tread on the serpent. (Luke 10:19)
I can tread Satan underfoot. (Rom. 16:20)
I cannot be moved. (Ps. 16:8)
I cannot be separated from God's love. (Rom. 8:35-39)
God loves me. (John 3:16)
I cannot be charged or accused. (Rom. 8:33)
I have a home in Heaven waiting for me. (John 14:1-2)
I have a sure hope. (Heb. 6:19)
I have authority over the enemy. (Luke 10:19)
I have access to the Father. (Rom. 5:2, Eph. 2:18)
I have mustard seed sized faith. (Luke 17:6)
I have power to witness. (Acts 1:8)

I have the mind of Christ. (1 Cor. 2:16)

I have shelter under His wings. (Ps. 91:1)

I have provision because God meets my needs. (Phil. 4:19)

I am a new creation in Christ. (2 Cor. 5:17)

I am who God says I am. (Rom. 3:4)

I am forgiven. (Mt. 26:28)

I am loved. (John. 3:16)

I am the head only, not the tail. (Dt. 28:13)

I am above only, not beneath. (Dt. 28:13)

I am blessed coming and I am blessed going. (Dt. 28:6)

I am filled with the Spirit. (Eph. 5:18)

I am blessed with every spiritual blessing. (Eph. 1:3)

I am the light of the world. (Mt. 5:14)

I hear God's voice. (John 10:27)

I cannot be taken out of my Father's hand. (John 10:29)

I will not be shaken. (Ps. 62:6)

I lack no good thing. (Ps. 34:10)

I am born again. (1 Pet. 1:23)

I am healed by His stripes. (Isa. 53:6)

I am hidden in the secret place of the Almighty. (Ps. 91:1)

I am secure in Christ. (John 10:28-29)

I am set on a Rock. (Ps. 40:2)

I am more than a conqueror. (Rom. 8:37)

I am kept by the power of God. (1 Pet. 1:5)

I am a believer, and the light of the Gospel shines in my mind. (2 Cor. 4:4)

I am a branch on Christ's vine. (John 15:5)

I am redeemed from the curse of the law. (Gal. 3:13)

I am protected from the evil one. (2 Thes. 3:3; 1 John 5:18)

I have grace, which He has freely given me. (Eph. 1:6)

I am the salt of the earth. (Matt. 5:13)

I am His sheep. (John 10:14)

I have peace with God. (Rom. 5:1, 10; 2 Cor. 5:19)

I have power, love, and a sound mind. (1 Tim. 1:7)

I have a mind that is in perfect peace. (Is. 26:3)

I have overcome the enemy because greater is He Who lives in me. (1 John 4:4)

Start It

The Achievable Proverbs 31 Woman

Proverbs 31 woman has always been something that I read and think – right? I won't be sewing my own clothes – I can **never** meet this standard of a woman. I will never measure up!

Until recently…. No, I didn't wake up today as SUPERwoman!

I realized that I had always looked at the Proverbs 31 woman comparing myself to her, this "perfect" woman, and seeing myself through eyes that could never measure up!

But… Today, I looked at Proverbs 31 in a new way. I saw it as if I WERE the Proverbs 31 woman. I rewrote it in my own "self-talk" as if I were already these things.

Really, I started speaking to my future self. Even where I didn't measure up to this standard, it was where I was going! Ladies, we may never arrive at having perfect performance. What's important is that we start! Start what? Sewing? No! We only need to see ourselves through the eyes of whom God has made us.

We need to speak to our future!

Experts suggest that what behavior you expect from your child, you will get. Isn't the same true for us? Low expectations breeds low performance.

Scripture says that we will eat the fruit of our lips. What are your lips speaking about you, your family, and your future? Are they filled with life and truth or death and lies?

You try it! Here is what I did:

- My husband and son-in-loves love Jesus and do not give not their strength to [loose] women, My daughters and I do not give our hearts or bodies to loose men – only to our husband's! (Prov. 31:2-3)
- Our family is called to influence and therefore, we will not drink so that our judgment is not impaired. (Prov. 31:4-7)
- I will care for the underdogs! I will teach them to fish, not merely feed them. (Prov. 31:8-9)
- I am a capable, intelligent & virtuous woman. I am more precious than rubies and pearls. (Prov. 31:10)
- My husband confidently trusts, relies, & believes in me. I have no lack. I comfort, encourage & do him only good – until I pass from this earth! (Prov. 31:11-12)
- I work hard. I am not lazy when it comes to caring for my family. I prepare for their meals. (Prov. 31:13-14)
- I rise early. ☺ First thing, I bring my family spiritual nourishment. I assign each member of my family (and worker) tasks. (Prov. 31:15)
- I am a suitable steward of what God has given me. I have the mind of Christ and wisdom from the Lord and I use it in every business & financial decision. I don't ignore my most important responsibilities. (Prov. 31:16)
- I encourage myself in the Lord and in Truth so I can be Spiritual minded rather than carnal minded. I am physically fit. My arms are strong and firm so that I have the life to carry out what God has called me to. (Prov. 31:17)
- The work of God in me I acknowledge and remember when hard times press around me. God's light continues to shine in trials of all kinds. (Prov. 31:18)
- I work hard. I feed others who are poor in Spirit. (Prov. 31:19-20)

- I have skills that benefit my family (like sewing, designing, etc. God will equip me with whatever skills I need). I dress as if I am an ambassador of Jesus Christ! (Prov. 31:21-22)
- My husband is known in the city's gates (in the nation's gates). He consults with the elders of all the lands – pastors, teachers, business leaders and the like. (Prov. 31:23)
- I write Bible studies, books, videos, skits, games and fun things to help Christ followers know who they are in Christ. I build up leaders, in my and future generations, to be a leader in their own circle. (Prov. 31:24)
- Strength and dignity are my clothing. My position is strong and secure. I rejoice over the future! My family is ready for it! (Prov. 31:25)
- My mouth is filled with Godly wisdom and my tongue is kind. I give counsel and instruction. (Prov. 31:26)
- I refuse to be idle! I am not discontent. I don't pity myself. I refuse to gossip. I look well to how things go in my home. (Prov. 31:27)
- My children will call me blessed. My daughter's hearts toward me are always pure.
- My husband boasts about and praises me. He thinks I am the cream of the crop. ☺ (Prov. 31:28-29)
- I fear the Lord. I worship the Lord. I am in awe of You Lord! (Prov. 31:30)
- What I sow, I will reap. My works will show the fruit of the Spirit - hopefully, not the fruit of my flesh! (Prov. 31:31)

Now, start speaking to your future and watch what God will do through your renewed mind!

I would love to hear your stories. Submit them to sheri@ikanministries.com

Love,
Sheri